AA POCKET GUIDE

MOROCCO

Books ar

Stevenson College
Bankhead Avenue
EDINBURGH EH11 4DE

Written by Barnaby Rogerson
Peace and Quiet section
by Paul Sterry
Original photography
by Paul Kenward

© The Automobile Association 1995
First published January 1992 as
Essential Morocco
Revised second edition January
1995
Reprinted November 1995
Reprinted as *Pocket Guide Morocco*
1999

Maps © The Automobile Association
1995

Published by AA Publishing, a
trading name of Automobile
Association Developments Limited,
whose registered office is Norfolk
House, Priestley Road, Basingstoke,
Hampshire RG24 9NY.
Registered number 1878835.

Distributed in the United Kingdom
by AA Publishing, Norfolk House,
Priestley Road, Basingstoke,
Hampshire RG24 9NY.

A CIP catalogue record for this book
is available from the British Library.

ISBN 0 7495 2127 9

The Automobile Association retains
the copyright in the original edition
© 1992 and in all subsequent
editions, reprints and amendments.

Colour separation: L C Repro Ltd,
Aldermaston

Printed by: Printer Trento srl, Italy

Front cover picture: *Meknes* (AA
Photo Library – I Burgum)

This book employs a simple rating system to help choose which places to visit:

✓ 'top ten'

◆◆◆ do not miss
◆◆   see if you can
◆   worth seeing if you have time

Country Distinguishing Signs
On the maps, international distinguishing signs indicate the location of countries around Morocco. Thus:

DZ = Algeria   RIM = Mauritania   E = Spain
RMM = Mali   P = Portugal

INTRODUCTION

Morocco is different. Though only a cannon shot from Spain, it is part of an entirely different world.

Its land and its people are full of surprises. It has a perennially startling landscape that can shift you from dense cedar forest to deserts, from an irrigated garden to a wall of mountains and take you down wide, meandering river beds to sublime white beaches. In Morocco you can ski not just on water, but also down

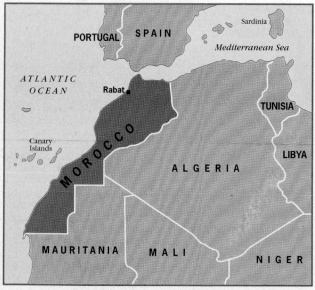

mountain snow and desert sand dunes.

Travelling here is like entering a time machine as you move from a sophisticated modern city on the Atlantic coast to almost medieval scenes in mountain villages and the streets of ancient cities.

Morocco is ruled by King Hassan II, a man who is typical in his blend of modernity and tradition. He is Commander of the Faithful and a descendant of the prophet Mohammed. He is also a fanatically keen sportsman.

Within seconds of Said Aouita winning an

Olympic gold medal for the 5,000 metres in 1984, he could be seen standing to attention and receiving a congratulatory radio telephone call. No one in Morocco doubted who was on the other end of the line.

Moghrebi Arabic is the national language with French used for big business and higher education. At home, about half the nation might speak one of the three ancient Berber dialects.

Morocco is also known as Maghreb el Aksa, the land of the furthest west. It is a part of the wider world of Islam and Africa but it also has a distinctive identity formed by its isolation on the far reaches of both these cultures. For Morocco, despite the evidence of the map, is encircled by three forbidding oceans. To the north by the Mediterranean, to the west by the Atlantic and to the south and east by the sand seas of the Sahara. This spirit of insular self sufficiency has been further exaggerated by four great mountain ranges that dissect the nation. The Rif mountains have acted like a wall that runs along the northern coast to keep Mediterranean influence at a minimum. The Middle (Moyen), High (Haut) and Anti-Atlas are a series of overlapping mountain ranges that shield the prosperous river valleys and coastal plains of central Morocco from the Sahara. This political and economic heartland of the nation has long been dominated by two rival cities of the interior. It was at Fès and Marrakech that the distinctive Moroccan national culture was first defined.

Their influence has waned during the last hundred years to be replaced by modern, more outward-looking cities on the Atlantic coast, like Rabat and Casablanca. The Atlas mountains are an invaluable barrier against the desert but in human terms they have acted more as a filter than a frontier. Due to the importance of the trans-Saharan gold trade they were a valuable part of the nation. They have also had a strong political role: none of the ruling dynasties of Morocco have originated from the prosperous centre. They have all come from the harsher lands, productive of a warlike temperament, to the south or east of the mountains.

INTRODUCTION

How to Use this Guide

Morocco has been divided into four regions (with Western Sahara included as part of the country) for the purpose of this guide. However, do not worry if you are already booked into one hotel for your entire holiday. Each area has more than enough to exhaust the most energetic tourist. There are mountains, beaches, bustling resorts and striking monuments to be seen in each of the regions, briefly described below.

Tanger and the North

It is difficult to find a balanced opinion about Tanger (Tangier), for the world seems to be divided between those who love it and those who loathe it. All, however, agree that it is both a cosmopolitan and mysterious city. It has a temperate Mediterranean climate and is blessed with a number of distinguished old hotels, fine restaurants and a lively nightlife. Mountain citadels, ancient caves, beaches, quiet fishing villages, ruined fortresses and old walled cities on the Atlantic and Mediterranean coasts are all within easy reach.

The Imperial Cities

The undramatic but fertile plains of central Morocco have always been the heartland of the nation and are littered with the monuments of this imperial past. All three principal cities, the current capital of Rabat, medieval Fès and 17th-century Meknès have served as national capitals at one time or another, and are guardians of the country's Islamic heritage. In addition there are refreshing beaches on the Atlantic coast, Roman ruins at Volubilis, a holy town at Moulay-Idriss, industrious, metropolitan Casablanca and cool hill stations in the Middle Atlas mountains.

Marrakech and the High Atlas

Red-walled Marrakech with its labyrinthine market, luxurious hotels, gardens and hectic central square is the most celebrated destination in the country. There is as much to see here as there is to buy. Rising like a mirage to the south of the city, the peaks of the

Once a great imperial city Meknès's political status has declined but its souk still thrives with trade

BACKGROUND

Prehistory

Africa is the origin of mankind. The rest of the world was innocent of man until a million years ago when *Homo erectus* first crossed the Sahara. Evidence of this stone- and fire-using human ancestor have been found in the area just south of Casablanca. By 40,000BC modern man had spread across the old world and had already divided into separate races. The retreat of the last Ice Age was complete by 10,000BC which allowed the Mediterranean to expand into its current dimensions and separate the population of North Africa from Europe.

The Neolithic revolution – the invention of agriculture and stock-keeping – reached Morocco in 3,000BC. It transformed the drifting groups of hunter-gatherers into settled communities and vastly increased the population. This enormous change was not by conquest but by a slow cultural dissemination that worked east along the seaboard. The indigenous people of North Africa are known as Berbers, a word of Greek origin, and the earliest records speak of their devotion to war, to polygamy, to their chariots and to their herds of sheep and goats.

A Roman provincial capital for over two hundred years, the ruins of the city of Volubilis evoke past glory

The Phoenicians and Romans

It was the Phoenician merchants of Lebanon that first introduced the higher arts of civilisation. They were the fairy godmothers of ancient Morocco, though their motives were entirely mercenary. By 1000BC they had established a permanent settlement at Tanger which was soon followed by other colonies down the Atlantic coast. From these centres the skills of metal-working, stone-carving, weaving, pottery and improved agriculture, with new varieties of crops, were disseminated. Carthage emerged as the leader of all the Phoenician colonies in the Western Mediterranean during the 6th century BC. From this period comes a description of the Carthaginian admiral Hanno's voyage of discovery down the coast to West Africa.

After the destruction of the city of Carthage in 146BC, Rome assumed the 'protection' of the scattered Phoenician colonies. The interior of North Africa was ruled by native kings whose territories were slowly annexed by Rome. Juba II, who ruled northern Morocco from his inland capital of Volubilis, was the last of these rulers to survive. He was a noted scholar who

had been educated in the household of the
Emperor Augustus, where he had met and
married the princess Silene, the daughter of
Mark Anthony and Cleopatra. Their son
Ptolemy was murdered by the Emperor
Caligula and their kingdom conquered in
AD44, during the reign of the Emperor
Claudius.

The province consisted of just the
northwestern coast and was not even
connected by road to Roman Algeria. When
the Baquates tribe overran the defences at the
end of the 3rd century the Empire decided to
restrict itself to holding the strategic city ports
of Tanger and Ceuta. Later powers like the
Vandals and Byzantines followed in their
footsteps, and left the fierce Berber tribes to
their own devices.

Islam and the Arab Invasion

This was all to be changed by a theocratic state
that had been established in the Arabian
peninsula. The prophet Mohammed died in
632 but the cavalry armies of his successors
soon conquered an enormous empire. In 682
Oqba ben Nafi made his legendary raid into
Morocco, riding deep into the Atlantic surf to
prove that there was no land any further west
to be conquered for Islam. Musa ben Noussir
organised a more thorough conquest of
Morocco between 705 and 710. He
established garrisons at Tanger and the Tafilalt
but it was soon made clear that his real
objective had been the conquest of Spain. The
only value Morocco held for the Arab
governors was as a source of slaves and
recruits for their army. In 740 the
disillusioned Berber soldiers in the Tanger
garrison assassinated their Arab
governor and revolted. They adopted a
rigorous puritanism in order to make a clear
distinction between their support of the Muslim
religion and the rejection of their Arab
overlords.

The Idrissids

Berber enthusiasm for the new religion was
further demonstrated in 789. Moulay Idriss, a
Kinsman of the prophet Mohammed, had fled

INTRODUCTION

to Morocco to escape the vengence of Harun al Rashid, the great Caliph of Baghdad. He was acclaimed ruler by the Berber tribes around Meknès but was poisoned by an agent of the Caliph two years later. Fortunately his Berber mistress was pregnant and gave birth to a son who later reigned as Idriss II. He ruled central Morocco and established Fès as a great bastion of Arab and Islamic culture. After his death in 828 his kingdom was divided among nine sons who have attained legendary status as missionary princes who brought the faith to far-flung provinces. Though the power of the Idrissids, the descendants of Idris II, soon waned, their spiritual prestige remains a strong and continual feature of Moroccan history.

The Almoravides, 1042–1147

By the 11th century Morocco had deteriorated into a patchwork of despotic petty states and feuding tribes with many of the chief ports and towns under the control of foreign powers. In the far reaches of the Western Sahara, a native scholar who had returned from Mecca determined to create a true Islamic state. His

Waves of sand undulate across the surface of the Sahara, Morocco's southern sea

vision and discipline, allied to the ferocity of
the Saharan tribes created a powerful force of
warriors of the faith – the Almoravides. They
emerged in 1042 and conquered an enormous
desert empire that stretched south to the Niger
river and north towards Morocco. This was to
be further extended by Youssef ben Tachfine,
an Almoravide general who established
Marrakech as his base camp in 1071. Within 20
years Youssef had conquered not only
Morocco but also the sophisticated city-states
of Muslim Spain. Skilled Andalucian craftsmen,
secretaries and architects were employed by
the Almoravide court and began to introduce
the higher civilisation of Moorish Spain into
Morocco.

The Almohads, 1147–1248

At the height of the Almoravide Empire, Ibn
Tumert, another native scholar, returned from
Mecca full of schemes to establish an even
more rigorous Islamic state. He established
himself at Tin-Mal in the High Atlas mountains
and created an obedient army from the Berber
highland tribes. Victory over the Almoravides
was achieved by his successor, Abdel
Moumen who established an empire that
stretched over Spain, Algeria, Tunisia and part
of Libya. It is the golden period of Moroccan
history, when Almohad fleets dominated the
Western Mediterranean and great
philosophers like Averroës received the full
support of the sultan's court. Some of the glory
is still reflected in the magnificent buildings
that adorn Rabat and Marrakech, like the
Koutoubia and El Hassan minarets and the
formal gates of Oudaïa and Aguenaou. A
crushing defeat in Spain, at Las Navas de
Tolosa in 1213, rocked imperial authority and
the sultans were faced with a series of
escalating revolts. In 1248 the Almohad sultan
died while on campaign on the Algerian
border, and his leaderless army was
massacred by the powerful Beni Merin tribe as
it struggled home. The tribal chiefs of the Beni
Merin promptly established their capital at Fès
but it took another 21 years of war before they
could destroy the last Almohad army that
defended Marrakech.

The Merenids, 1248–1554

The reigns of Sultan Abou Hassan, 1331–51 and his son Abou Inan, 1351–58 are the zenith of the long centuries of Merenid rule. In this period Merenid armies twice occupied Tunis and seemed at the point of restoring the unity of the Almohad Empire. The Merenid architecture of the 14th century, particularly the **medersas** (schools for Koranic studies) that can be seen in Fès, Meknès and Salé testify to the exquisite taste of the sultans and their generous patronage of religious learning. The works of Ibn Battuta, 'the Muslim Marco Polo', and Ibn Khaldoun, one of the world's greatest historians, are proof of the lively intellectual life of the period.

Wealth poured into the state coffers from the enormously profitable trans-Saharan caravan trade in gold, precious oils and ivory.

The period finished in 1358, when Sultan Abou Inan was smothered with a pillow by his vizier as he lay recovering from an illness.

This royal murder is a parable for the gradual decline of the state. The sultans became mere figureheads as real power fell into the hands of a corrupt coterie of viziers, financiers and generals. In the 15th century the expansionist Portuguese kingdom began to seize control of a number of Moroccan ports which the Merenids proved powerless to hold. By the mid-16th century the Portuguese were in almost complete control of the coastline and in 1578 the boy king, Sebastian, attempted outright conquest.

The Saadians, 1554–1668

The inability of the Merenid rulers to oppose the Portuguese allowed for the rise of a number of local war leaders. The most effective of these were the Saadians who organised the siege of Agadir in 1510. This Portuguese fort finally fell in 1542, by which time the Saadians were already well established in Marrakech as the rulers of southern Morocco. Seven years later they were strong enough to capture the Merenid capital of Fès. In 1578 the Saadian dynasty won eternal fame with the crushing defeat of the Portuguese invasion at the battle of Ksar-el-Kebir. Sultan Abdel Malik died in the hour of

Mountain tribesmen who now tend their sheep, once played a central rôle in the country's turbulent history

victory and his brother Ahmed inherited the throne and took the title El Mansour – 'the victorious'. He gained additional fame by the conquest of Timbuctoo whose treasure gave him another epithet – El Dhabbi, 'the golden one'.

Surviving memorials of Ahmed's reign include the glittering Saadian tombs and the ruins of the palace of El Badia in Marrakech. His sons destroyed their inheritance in a furious succession war and discredited the dynasty by selling the port of Larache in 1610 to the Christians. Though a number of Saadian princes lived on in splendour at Marrakech, real authority was exercised elsewhere. A three-cornered fight developed between petty dynasties based on the Rif, Anti-Atlas and Middle Atlas mountains. However, after 40 years of warfare, power fell into the hands of Moulay Rachid, a young prince of holy lineage whose Alouite family came from the oasis of Tafilalt. Within four years of raising his standard at Taza he had seized complete control of the country. He ruled for just four years and was succeeded by his younger brother, Moulay Ismaïl.

Moulay Ismaïl, 1672–1727

Certain monarchs breed legends and the reign of Moulay Ismaïl has always been in danger of being overwhelmed by stories of his cruelty and sexual prowess. He was undoubtedly fertile and tyrannical but his long reign was also a period of great achievement. He reformed the nation's cult-ridden religious life, disciplined the Berber mountain tribes, liberated Tanger from the English and Larache, Asilah and Mehdiya from the Spanish. The imperial city at Meknès was built in this period but there are many other testaments to his energy: the bridges, kasbahs and markets that he built throughout the country and the numerous mosques, palaces and walls that he had restored. It was the proud boast of his reign that the roads were safe enough for a woman or a Jew to travel across the breadth of the country without being troubled. This unaccustomed order was only achieved by an authoritarian regime backed by a standing army of 150,000 Negro slaves. His failure, and it was a great one, was not to delegate authority to any of his many

Sunset over Maghreb el Aksa, the land furthest west

sons. His death was followed by a 20-year war as his regiments and heirs struggled for dominance.

Decline in the 18th and 19th Centuries

None of the immediate descendants of Moulay Ismaïl was to match the great sultan's power. Their authority was in practice restricted to the coastal plains and river valleys, the area which was known as the Bled-el-Makhzen, the land of government, while the mountainous areas of tribal power were known as the Bled-es-Siba, the land of dissidence. Sidi Mohammed (1757–1790) was one of the most astute sultans of this period whose reign is well represented by the elegant port of Essaouira which he founded.

The 19th century was a period of increasing European power, graphically demonstrated by the French invasion of Algeria in 1830. After 1856, European merchants in Morocco were running their own law courts while their coinages began to displace the native currency. By the turn of the century the two chief ports of Tanger and Casablanca were effectively under the control of the foreign consuls. Despite the reforms attempted by Sultan Moulay Hassan (1873–94) the country slipped ever more under debt and European influence.

The French Protectorate

The rivalry over Morocco between the European powers was settled by secret negotiations at the 1906 conference of Algeciras. France was given central Morocco and Spain the poorer areas in the extreme south and north. The next year French troops landed at Casablanca. Several years of confused fighting and diplomacy was resolved in 1912 when the sultan signed away sovereignty through the treaty of Fès. Later that year the tribal army of El Hiba, the Blue Sultan of the desert, was destroyed outside Marrakech. The French immediately began work on the colonial transformation of 'Maroc Utile' – 'useful Morocco'. The less rewarding mountain regions were not completely pacified until 1934 and the 1921–26 Rif rebellion nearly succeeded in expelling the Spanish from the north of the country.

The technical achievements of the 44 years of colonial rule were impressive. A complete road and rail network was established, and ports, airfields, dams, irrigation projects and new administrative centres were created. The rewards of this new society – the hotels, hospitals and schools – were reserved for the 300,000 European settlers and the traditional Moroccan ruling class.

Independent Morocco

By 1947 the more ugly aspects of French colonial rule were being questioned by Sultan Mohammed V and the Istiqal, a small independence party. By 1951 both the Sultan and the rapidly expanding Istiqal were working to awaken the political life of the nation. This was dramatically achieved in 1953 when the French deposed Mohammed V and sent him into exile in Madagascar. In 1955 the mass demonstrations for his return had begun to escalate into a guerrilla war. The French government, which was then faced with a revolution in Algeria, decided to quit Morocco with grace. Mohammed V returned and by March 1956 had formally negotiated independence. He changed his title from sultan to king and his enormous popularity helped him outmanoeuvre the party bosses and remain the dominant political figure. He was succeeded in 1961 by his son Hassan II. In the succeeding three decades parties, constitutions, crises, coups and cabinets have come and gone but the king remains very much in charge. Successes like the smooth nationalisation of foreign businesses in 1965 and the Maghrebi Union treaty of 1989 are eclipsed by the Green March of 1975 which is by far the most popular achievement of his reign. As General Franco of Spain lay dying the king led 350,000 unarmed Moroccans across the southern frontier to lay claim to the Spanish held Western Sahara. This enormous territory is now integrated into Morocco and the long guerilla war against the Polisario movement has now been replaced by a United Nations monitored truce.

TANGER AND THE NORTH

The old international city of Tanger (Tangier) is the natural centre for exploring the north of Morocco. Tanger has a busy beach, lined with fish restaurants and tapas bars. It has the liveliest nightlife and the most varied selection of restaurants in the country. Shopping expeditions in the alleys of the old town and a visit to the museum in the kasbah quarter make an excellent introduction to Moroccan culture.

Daytrips out of town might begin with the surrounding beaches at **Malabata**, **Ksar-es-Seghir** and the **Grottes d'Hercule** (**Caves of Hercules**). **Asilah**, about an hour's drive due south from Tanger, is just that bit further removed. With its charming Portuguese ramparts, local market and fishing port, it is deservedly popular. **Tetouan**, with its two museums and labyrinthine medina (walled town), or the Spanish outpost of **Ceuta** are more demanding destinations, though an early start could leave the afternoon free for basking in the calm waters of the Mediterranean. **Chechaouen**, a whitewashed citadel tucked into the Rif mountains, three hours from Tanger, deserves more than a passing visit. Staying for a night, you can use the cool of the evening and morning for short hikes into the surrounding hills. To the east, the mountains are bleaker and less rewarding, with dramatic features at **Ketama** and **Beni-Snassen** and reclusive beaches at **Saidia** and **Al-Hoceima**.

Shadows and lights, Tanger's harbour

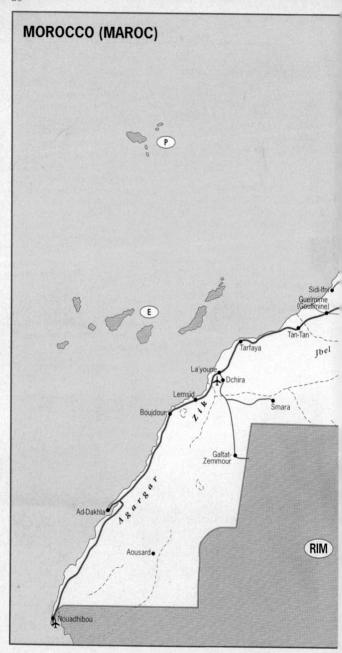

MOROCCO (MAROC)

P

Sidi-Ifni

Guelmime
(Goulimine)

E

Tan-Tan

Jbel

Tarfaya

La'youne

Dchira

Lemsid

Smara

Boujdour

Z i k

Galtat-
Zemmour

A g a r g a r

Ad-Dakhla

RIM

Aousard

Nouadhibou

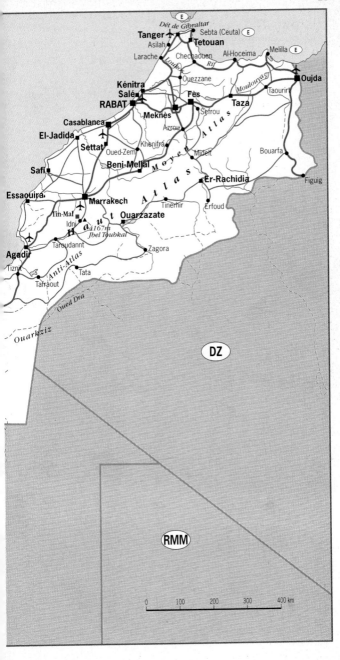

TANGER

Tanger, a city of 300,000 inhabitants, is spread over low hills and overlooks a wide bay washed by both the Atlantic and the Mediterranean. Similarly, on land Tanger is also a meeting point – for the separate cultures of Islamic North Africa and Christian Europe. For the first half of this century it was an international city, misruled by a council of consuls who allowed it to develop as a centre for smugglers, spies, shady financiers, exiles and homosexuals. A touch of this heady and exotic air remains. Old Tanger is the medina, the walled Arab town with its maze of narrow alleys. The new town is to the south of this, off boulevards Pasteur and Mohammed V, with most of the hotels, restaurants and bars.

WHAT TO SEE

◆
AMERICAN LEGATION
8 rue America
This, the oldest American consulate in the world, complete with its period 19th-century furniture, portraits, library and map room, is now a quiet museum. It periodically holds exhibitions of the work of contemporary Moroccan artists. The garden courtyards extend on either side of the medina alley, its entrance just after the covered archway off rue du Portugal in the southern corner of the medina.
Open: Monday, Wednesday, Thursday 10.00–13.00 and 15.00–17.00 hrs, other times by appointment.

◆◆◆
KASBAH and DAR EL MAKHZEN ✓

The kasbah, the high ground to the west of the medina, was completely rebuilt by Sultan Moulay Ismaïl after the English abandoned Tanger in 1685. The **Mechouar**, its central paved square, is overlooked by the old prison, treasury and law court. **Bab er Raha** gate guards a terrace that catches the coastal winds while **Bab el Aissa**, the gate of watchfulness, leads into the medina.
The Dar el Makhzen, the palace of the governor, has been turned into a museum of traditional crafts. The internal architecture and the enclosed Andalucian garden vie with the actual exhibits for your attention, but keep a look-out for the ceramic collection, the strong boxes of the treasury and the illuminated Korans. The archaelogical department boasts a mosiac of Venus and copies of the Volubilis bronze busts.
Open: Wednesday to Monday 09.00–12.00 hrs and 15.00–18.00 hrs in summer, 09.00–15.30 hrs in winter. Closed Tuesdays.

◆◆
MÉDINA
On your first visit to the twisted alleys of the old quarter, hire an official guide from the office at 29 boulevard Pasteur. Otherwise take the right hand of the two **Grand Socco** arches which leads directly into rue es Siaghin, the

Timeless bustle in the streets

silversmiths' street, which with rue des Chrétiens is the busiest shopping alley in the old town. Promenade downhill, passing the old Jewish quarter on your right and then a disused Catholic church before reaching a small square, fringed with cafés and hotels, known as the **Petit Socco**. In Roman times this was the forum of their city, Tingis, and in more recent history it was the centre of Tanger's vice trade. Take rue de la Marine past the 17th century Grande Mosquée, built by Sultan Moulay Ismaïl, to reach **Bordj el Marsa**, the port battery which has been made into a viewing terrace. From there, the Bab el Bahr steps take you out of the old city to the port gates and the long beach promenade.

◆
PALAIS MENDOUB (MUSEUM OF MILITARY MINIATURES)
Marshan

Malcolm Forbes, the American millionaire publisher who created a stir by flying 700 'friends' and 110 journalists out to Tanger for his 70th birthday co-hosted by Elizabeth Taylor, owns this charming old palace of the Sultan's representative. His party cost $2 million by the way, and generated a massive 20,000 news clippings.

In keeping with this eccentric behaviour, Forbes has turned part of the palace into a museum of toy soldiers and militaria. The display is complemented by a terraced garden and a fine view out to Cape Trafalgar.

Open: daily 10.00–17.00 hrs. Admission free but tips welcomed.

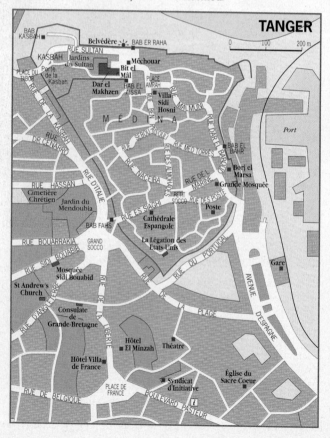

◆◆
PLACE DE FRANCE and the GRAND SOCCO

Tanger seems to have been designed for café-life, and both new and old towns are equipped with two bustling areas, lined with tables and darting waiters.

The place de France, overlooked by the imposing garden of the French consulate, lies at the centre of the new town. From it the broad boulevard Pasteur/avenue Mohammed V descends east parallel to the beach, passing through a grid of regular streets lined with a variety of restaurants, bars, nightclubs, offices and shops.

The **Grand Socco**, the great market, is down rue de la Liberté from place de France. It is filled with local farmers' wives, selling their produce beneath distinctive broad-brimmed pompom hats, taxi ranks, buses, donkey carts and porters. Hidden behind are numerous covered markets, stalls and cheap native cafés, all overlooked by the richly tiled, slender minaret of the **Mosquée Sidi Bouabid**. Opposite the mosque there is a low green door into the **Jardin du Mendoubia**, with its enormous banyan tree and collection of 18th-century cannons. Above the mosque is an Anglican church (St Andrew's) whose Moorish interior includes the Lord's Prayer carved in Arabic script above the chancel. In the surrounding graveyard you can hunt out memorials to the exotic turn-of-the-century British community which included Emily, the Sherifa of Wazzan, Caid Maclean, a Scottish officer who took

Minaret of the Mosquée Sidi Bouabid towering over the faithful

service in the Sultan's army, Walter Harris, the writer and adventurer, and the powerful 19th-century British consul and friend of Sultan Moulay Hassan, Sir John Drummond Hay.

Accommodation

The **El Minzah Hotel** at 85 rue de la Liberté (tel: (09) 938787) is the most celebrated hotel in Tanger, with cool courtyards, a choice of restaurants and the smart Caid's Bar. Five stars. The three-star **Hotel Chellah** at

49 rue Allal ben Abdallah (tel: (09) 942003) and four-star **Hotel Tanjah Flandria** at 6 boulevard Mohammed V (tel: (09) 933300), are centrally placed for the new town nightclubs.

If you want to be on the beach, the **Hotel Solazur** on avenue des FAR (tel: (09) 940166) sits imposingly on the far eastern edge of town. Four stars.

For a combination of town, style and beachfront try **Hotel Rif** on avenue d'Espagne (tel: (09) 935910). Four stars. You could also consider the **Passadena** (tel: (09) 945915) which is set in its own elegant garden out of town on the road to Tetouan. Four stars.

If you are trying to keep to a tight budget look at the small beachfront hotels like the **Biarritz** (one star), **Miramar** (two stars) and **Valencia** and **Bretagne** on avenue des FAR before trying some of the pensions on rue du Portugal.

Restaurants

There is an amusing and raffish line of tapas bars and fish grills along the beachfront, producing snacks throughout the day and well into the night. For a longer, traditional Moroccan meal in a Moorish interior with music and belly-dancers, try the **Damascus Restaurant**, rue Prince Moulay Abdullah.

In the old town you will also find **Restaurant Hammadi** on rue de la Kasbah, the **Ibn Batouta** on rue es Siaghin and **Marhaba** at 67 place Ahannar.

There is a large choice of French, Spanish, Italian and Oriental restaurants to be sniffed out in the streets off boulevard Pasteur. English food is available, at **Emma's BBC Bar** on the beach.

Nightlife

Tanger's large hotels, the Africa, the Almohades, the Rif Hotel Sheherezade, all have their own nightclubs, but the most lively and sophisticated by far is Hotel Tanjah Flandria's '**Le Palais**'. There is also a string of independent discothèques along rue Moutanabi and rue Prince Moulay Abdullah, which you can intersperse with Moroccan cabaret at the **Koutoubia Palace** and **Morocco Palace**.

Shopping

Before plunging into the bazaars of the old town have a look at the craft showrooms on rue de Belgique, to get your eye in.

On rue de la Liberté in the new town, have a look at the Tindouf antique shops. There is a good bookshop at 54 boulevard Pasteur and the famous Madini perfumery at 14 rue Sebou in the medina, where dozens of different perfumes are made up to secret family recipes.

Special Events

In July, the unlikely sounding **Detroit Music Festival** takes place in Tanger. However, September is the most fashionable month, when the *moussem* (festival) of **Dar Zhirou** and **International Week** both occur.

WHAT TO SEE IN THE NORTH

AL-HOCEIMA
203 miles (327km) from Tanger
After the suppression of a local rebellion in 1926, the Spanish built the town of Al-Hoceima as a modern administrative centre for their protectorate in the northern Rif mountains. Half way along the Moroccan Mediterranean coast, its regular avenues of white houses cascade down to a small, cliff-fringed beach now dominated by three tourist hotels. It is a friendly place, its isolation somewhat offset by a local airport which has made it into a peaceful and unusual beach resort.

The most famous local site is the offshore Spanish island of **Peñon de Alhucemas**. At night this inaccessible outpost is lit up and appears like a ship lying out to anchor. It has held a garrison since 1673, falling briefly to Abdel Krim, the local hero who led the 1926 rising. The tourist office arranges regular trips to nearby local markets.

Accommodation
Hotel Quemado (tel: (09) 982371) is the best of the three almost identical hotels. Three stars.

ASILAH
28 miles (46km) south of Tanger
The fishing port of Asilah makes a refreshing contrast to the busy city. It is a small, quiet town, with a whitewashed old quarter contained within 16th-

Finding time to stop and stare

Local traffic: a beast and its burden

century Portuguese walls, and a beautiful long beach that stretches to the north.

A walk through the old town begins near the restaurants at **Bab el Bahr**, the sea gate. Pass below the tower to reach the seafront promenade. Half way along is the town's chief site, the restored Portuguese Moorish **palace of Raisuli** (unfortunately no longer open to visitors). The Caid Raisuli was a celebrated figure of pre-colonial Morocco, a curious mixture of bandit, saint, freedom fighter and tyrant. The palace was built in 1906 when he was the virtual viceroy of the north, a position

he achieved by kidnapping a Greek-American millionaire. In the southern corner of the town is the **tomb, pier and cemetery of Sidi Mansur**. The blue-hued whitewash, the weathered stone of the walls and the neatly tiled tombs make it a favourite subject for painters. Wind your way through back alleys to **Bab Homar**, the land gate, where the local farmers still hold their market. On the way you will pass a startling series of modern **murals** produced during the annual Intellectual Festival in August.

Accommodation and Eating

Asilah is best known for its half-dozen popular campsites by the railway station. They are well organised and open straight on to the Atlantic beach.

In the same area is the swish **Al Khaima Hotel** (tel: (09) 917234). Three stars. The **Oued Makhazine Hotel** on rue Melilla (tel: (09) 917090) makes a cheaper mid-town alternative. One star.

Treat yourself to a drink or a meal at **El Oceano** restaurant which sits pleasantly shaded by ramparts on the corner of place Zallach.

◆
BENI-SNASSEN MOUNTAINS

This delightful group of forested hills cut through with streams and the Zegzel gorge (Gorges du Zegzel) is isolated from the main body of the Rif mountains in the middle of the eastern plain. Signposted mountain tracks allow cars to reach the **Grotte du Chameau** with its hot mineral spring and underground stalactite halls as well as the **Pigeon Cave**, a famous Neolithic burial site, and also offer a more adventurous drive right through the **Zegzel gorge**. The hills are named after the Beni Snassen Berbers who fiercely resisted the French invasion. At length the tribal chiefs were forced to surrender but they planned their revenge by staging a great feast of wild boar in honour of the French colonel. It was a quiet revenge, for the colonel was completely unaware that for a Muslim to serve pigmeat to a guest is one of the gravest of insults.

CEUTA (SEBTA)

23 miles (38km) north of Tetouan
The promontory mountains of Ceuta and Gibraltar that guard the narrow entrance to the Mediterranean have been known since ancient times as the Pillars of Hercules. They have a colourful history, and just as Gibraltar has been proudly British for 300 years, so the ferry port of Ceuta, on the North African shore, never fails to remind you of its 500-year history as a Spanish fortress.

The Moroccan Customs officers show their resentment in a sometimes deliberately slow border-crossing procedure. The massive bougainvillaea-draped 16th-century ramparts, the plaza de Africa with its church of Our Lady of Africa, the monumental town hall and the Catholic cathedral are all worth the inconvenience. There are also two museums of interest in Ceuta. The **Museu de la Legion** on Paseo de Colón catalogues the activities of the Spanish Foreign Legion. *Open*: weekends, 11.00–14.00 and 16.00–18.00 hrs.

In front of the port is the small **Museum of Antiquities**. *Open*: Tuesday to Sunday 09.00–13.00 and 17.00–19.00 hrs. Closed on Mondays.

Accommodation and Eating

When in Ceuta, stay on plaza de Africa. The four-star **Hotel Muralla** (tel: – via Spain – (34-956) 514940) is the best choice, and the popular **La Torre** restaurant is at No 15.

◆◆◆
CHECHAOUEN

(also spelt Xaouen or Chaouen)
37 miles (60km) south of Tetouan

Muslim refugees fled from Spain in the 15th century and built a replica of their Andalucian home in the Moroccan mountains. This walled, crescent-shaped town remained unchanged and hidden from Christian eyes until 1920. It is now a friendly market town which doubles as a popular stop-off for hillwalkers. **Uta al Hammam** is the café-lined central square at the heart of a maze of streets in the old town. It is overlooked by the octagonal minaret of the **Great Mosque** and the kasbah's **Tower of Homage**. A museum of local crafts has been collected within the **kasbah**, which also boasts the perennial attractions of a garden, dungeon and secret underground tunnels.
Narrow avenue Hassan II, the principal shopping thoroughfare, leads downhill from Uta al Hammam to Bab el Ain, below which a market is held on Monday and Thursday.

Accommodation
The **Hotel Asma**, Sidi Abdelhamid (tel: (09) 986265) is an eyesore but it does have an excellent view over the town, a pool and an air of quiet seclusion. Three stars. Otherwise try the **Hotel de Chaouen**, also known as the Parador, on place el Makhzen (tel: (09) 986324), perched on the edge of the medina but overlooking open countryside. Four stars.
Along rue Tarik ibn Ziad you will find cheaper hotels like the **Rif** (one star) and the **Magou** (two stars), and there are half a dozen pensions, popular with backpackers, in the old town.

◆◆
GROTTES D'HERCULE
10 miles (16km) west of Tanger

The coast to the west of Tanger is a favourite excursion. A round tour takes you through the Montagne, a smart garden suburb studded with royal palaces, before twisting through pine woods to reach the lighthouse at Cap Spartel. This was known to the Romans as Ampelusium, cape of wines. There are a number of rocky coves, sheltering beaches and beach bars before you reach the Cave of Hercules. This natural sea cave, through which the Atlantic pounds, has been augmented by thousands of years of quarrying. A guide will illuminate the rock walls to reveal great scallop-like grooves formed by cutting out individual millstones. Just up from the beach, below the cave, are the scant ruins of Roman Cotta dating from the 2nd century AD.

Accommodation
Beside the cave there are the seaview terraces of **Café Robinson** where you can hire fishing rods, horses and camels. There is also a campsite of the same name and **Les Grottes d'Hercule** hotel complex (tel: (09) 938765). Three stars.

A guiding light of maritime Morocco

◆
KETAMA
south of Chechaouen
In the centre of the Rif mountains is a small market town of Ketama which is surrounded by pine woods and overlooked by the volcano-like silhouette of Jbel (Mount) Tidiquin. The peak at 8,058 feet (2,456m) is touched with snow for half the year, which attracts occasional groups of rough skiers and langläufers (cross-country skiers). It was also a popular hillwalking station in the more innocent days of the Spanish Protectorate.
Now, however, it is unwise to visit Ketama other than as part of an organised group, for Ketama has become the centre for 'business'. In this region this means the illicit trade in marijuana. Farmers in the Rif mountains grow the common Indian hemp which is harvested in July. The flowers and young leaves are gathered and cut up to make the tobacco-like kif which is surreptitiously smoked in thin pipes throughout the north of Morocco. Hemp pollen is made into resin, which is the chief item of the export trade. The local brands like Ketama Gold and Triple Zero are spoken of with respect by drug dealers and aficionados. It is harvested by beating the plants inside cloth-lined tents; the sticky residue is then collected and hand pressed into kilo blocks. Additional forms of marijuana include a concentrated oil extract and an edible fudge known as *maajoun*.

The mountain road south from Ketama to Fès, the route de L'Unité, is one of the most dramatic drives in the country. It follows the old medieval trading route that connected Fès to the Mediterranean port of Badis. It was built by voluntary-labour battalions immediately after independence to connect the separate road systems of the French and Spanish Protectorates.

Accommodation

The **Tidighine** (tel: 16 – through the post office) is the only safe and comfortable hotel in Ketama. It has a swimming-pool, garden, tennis court and restaurant. Three stars.

LARACHE and LIXUS

about 60 miles (96km) south of Tanger

The wide serpentine bends of the River Loukos separate the modern town of Larache, south of Asilah, from **ancient Lixus**, where a resident guardian escorts visitors around the ruins. The tour begins at the storage tanks of the Roman port, now by the road, before moving uphill to admire the mosaic of Oceanus, God of the Sea, in the public baths. Near by is the theatre which was later converted into an amphitheatre. On top of the hill lie the confused ruins of a walled acropolis where, way before the Romans, a great sanctuary to the Phoenician god, Melkarth, once stood, surrounded by seven further temples.

In Larache, the circular **place de la Libération**, lined with cafés and hotels, and the El Pozo bar, still conjure up the period of Spanish influence. Traces of the town's confused and long history are also preserved in the **medina**, entered through Bab el Khemis. On the edge of this medina are a number of minor monuments including the ruins of **Kelibat fortress**, the **Kasbah de la Cigogne**, a 16th-century Saadian **fort** and a small **archaeological museum** established in a restored 15th-century Portuguese fort.

Accommodation

Hotel Riad is on rue Mohammed ben Abdellah (tel: (09) 912626). The old garden villa of the Duchess of Guise, has been turned into a delightful hotel, with a swimming pool and a restaurant. Two stars.

MALABATA

east of Tanger

The Tanger bay strectches east to produce another good area of sandy beach at Malabata. Here lie the ruins of a Portuguese fort and a Club Med Hotel occupies a garden created by Walter Harris, a turn-of-the-century British journalist-cum-daredevil. An elaborate folly, now a farmhouse, squats beside the Malabata lighthouse. Further east, a series of isolated sandy bays culminate at **Ksar-es-Seghir**, where a ruined 16th-century Portuguese fortress is drowning in sand dunes.

◆ MELILLA

northeast coast, about 75 miles (120km) from Algerian border
There is a regular car ferry from this Spanish outpost in Morocco (since 1497) to Malaga and Almeria in Spain. Few tourists find Melilla worth the possible delays and inevitable paperwork of the border crossing. However, if you are passing through you can wander through the streets and decaying walls of the 16th-century citadel where there is a small army-run **museum** in the bastion Concepcion.
Open: 09.00–13.00 and 16.00–18.00 hrs; closed Monday and Friday.
Then you can promenade under the shade of palm trees in the formal **Hernandez garden** between eating tapas at the **Metropol** bar which overlooks plaza España.

The castellated folly at Cape Malabata

◆◆ MOULAY BOUSSELHAM and ARBAOUA

about 85 miles (135km) south of Tanger
Arbaoua is a small hamlet just off the main Rabat to Tanger road. It is surrounded by pine woods and its principal feature is a hunting lodge, the two-star **Hotel Route de France** (tel: (07) 902608). The massive wooden fittings of its mock-Alpine interior are decorated with sporting trophies from the large hunting preserve that the hotel runs. A road runs west beside the preserve to reach the coastal **shrine of Moulay Bousselham** which is the object of a religious festival in the summer. The holy man was a 10th-century Egyptian Sufi. There is also a delightful sandy beach, a brackish lagoon visited by flamingos and **Le Lagon**, a quiet hotel with a swimming-pool and restaurant (tel: (07) 902603). Three stars.

The five pointed Moroccan star

◆
OUEZZANE
37 miles (60km) southwest of Chechaouen

This pretty highland market town is famous throughout Morocco for its fine olive oil. The town is spread like a wide crescent around the lower slopes of Jbel (Mount) bou-Hellal. It was founded in the 18th century by a religious teacher of distinguished Idrissid ancestry. Ouezzane rapidly became the religious centre of the region and its hereditary Sherifs (descendants of the Prophet) became influential figures in the politics of the north. The souks, mosques and cobbled streets of the old town extend above the conspicuous clock tower in the central place de L'Indépendence. It is well placed if you are travelling between Chechaouen and Fès, especially if your passing visit coincides with the Thursday morning market.

◆
OUJDA
northeast Morocco, on the Algerian border

The Bab el Wahab, the odd portions of city wall and the souk of the old town of Oujda are pretty enough but only a slight attraction when compared to the glories of Morocco's other old cities. Most foreign visitors who come east to this prosperous, tranquil city are on their way to the Algerian border or are using it as a convenient base for exploring the Beni-Snassen mountains and Saïdia beach.

Accommodation

The **Terminus**, by the railway station at place de L'Unité Africaine (tel: (06) 683211), is the oldest and most popular hotel in Oujda with its swimming-pool, restaurant and bar. Four stars.

For those on a tighter budget, try the nearby **Lutetia** at 44 boulevard Hassan el Oukil (tel: (06) 683365), with its intact interior of the 1950s. Two stars.

◆◆
RIF COAST

The long strip of sandy Mediterranean coast between Ceuta and Tetouan, backed by the Djeballa mountains, is being developed.

Smir Restinga is a new resort of little more than half a dozen large hotels spaced along a clear, cool waterline. Waterskiing and underwater fishing are both popular.

Mdiq has as its core an active fishing harbour, while just round the headland **Cabo Negro** is the most exclusively European enclave. It has two Club Med Hotels, a topless beach zone, a clutch of restaurants and a riding club. **Martil**, an old corsair port with an 18th-century kasbah, functions as a beach suburb for Tetouanis in the summer. **Oued Laou**, with a pebble beach and a simple campsite marks the end of this stretch. Further east the increasingly cliff-fringed shore is severely offset by a lack of hotels and a predominance of bandits and marijuana smugglers.

Accommodation
Try the four-star **Golden Beach Hotel** (tel: (09) 966477) at Mdiq, the **Kabila** (tel: (09) 975013) or the **Karabo** (tel: (09) 977070) or book yourself in advance into the holiday village Club Med Yasmina at Cabo Negro.

◆
SAÏDIA
37 miles (60km) north of Oujda
Six miles (10km) of sandy Mediterranean beach stretches between the Moulouya river estuary and the town of Saïdia, which perches on the Algerian border. Though there are development plans afoot it remains very much a Moroccan resort with its holiday chalets, campsites and four small hotels dominated by a lively bar life. The quiet beach backed by a wood and marshland nature preserve attracts a few of the more self-contained European tourists who often find it as convenient to stay at Oujda.

◆◆◆
TETOUAN

35 miles (57km) southeast of Tanger
Tetouan, 'the daughter of Granada', was founded at the end of the 15th century by refugees fleeing from the Christian conquest of the last Muslim kingdom of Spain. It grew rich on the back of the corsair fleet which operated from the nearby port at Martil. Tetouan and the neighbouring Spanish fort at Ceuta were destined to be rivals, and Tetouan was the site of a fierce Moroccan-Spanish battle in 1863. It was chosen to become the capital of the small Spanish protectorate in northern Morocco in 1913, and an elegant new town was built beside the walled city.

Sightseeing
New Town
The length of rue Mohammed V leads through the new town. At its centre is **place Moulay el Mehdi**, lined with banks, the post office and a still functioning Catholic church. Walk east to pass through the triangular **place el Yalaa** where there is a display of European cannon captured by Tetouani corsairs in the 17th century. Just to the north is the **Archaeological Museum**, its mature garden scattered with antiques, and a fine series of mosaics from **Lixus** (see page 32) and small bronzes indoors.
Open: 09.00–12.00 hrs and 14.00–18.00 hrs. Closed Tuesdays and Sundays.
Place Hassan, a large

ornamental square overlooked by the royal palace, divides the old city from the new town.

The Médina

Guides for a tour of this labyrinthine old quarter can be hired at the Tourist Office at 30 avenue Mohammed V. The medina is packed with mosques, secretive townhouses, arch-spanned alleyways, its walled perimeter punctuated by a series of ancient gates which you could not hope to find on your own. Ask in particular to be shown the colourful market squares, Souk el Hots, Guersa el Kebir, the long thoroughfare of the Souk el Foki and the calmer place de l'Oussa. Also worth a look are the pretty minaret of the **Sidi Saidi mosque** by the gate of that name, the rampart-fringed **Jardin Moulay Rachid** below Bab Remouz, and **Bab Ceuta**, with its view over the Muslim cemetery and the old Jewish quarter, **the mellah**. There is a striking difference between the Jewish and Muslim areas of the city. The Jewish houses are hung with first-floor iron balconies, where the Jewish ladies would sit while their Muslim counterparts were confined to their houses. Outside Bab el Okhla is a **School of Traditional Arts**, where students are trained in crafts such as mosaic-making, and show off their skills to visitors.
Open: 09.00–12.00 and 15.00–17.00 hrs. Closed Sundays, Tuesdays and August. Just within the gate the **Ethnographic Museum** holds a sumptuous display of traditional clothing, saddlery, kitchenware and armaments. Marriage trousseaux show some of the most brilliant workmanship.
Open: 08.30–12.00 hrs and 14.30–18.00 hrs. Closed Tuesdays.

All tours of Tetouan inevitably conclude at the **Brishka Palace**, an enormous carpet bazaar, formerly a Muslim merchant's house, where you can admire and buy a dazzling range of killims (woven carpets) and prayer rugs while sipping mint tea in a splendid turn-of-the-century Moorish interior.

Accommodation

Hotel Safir on avenue Kennedy, the road to Ceuta (tel: (09) 970144), is an elaborate hotel with all modern facilities. Four stars.

There are also a number of smaller, cheaper and more central hotels along rue Mohammed ben Larbi Torres. The **National** at no 8 (tel: (09) 963290) is an old, quiet place with a calm interior courtyard and a café. One star.

Restaurants

Restaurant Zerhoun at 7 boulevard Mohammed ben Larbi Torres (tel: (09) 966661) is friendly, and offers the unusual combination of a tapas bar and a shadowy Moorish dining room. Cheaper, and a good lunchtime haunt, is the **Café Moderne** at 1 Pasaje Achaach, between avenue Mohammed V and avenue Mohammed Torres.

THE IMPERIAL CITIES

The cities of Rabat, Meknès and Fès have all, at one time or another, served as imperial capitals. Ideally your itinerary should allow a couple of nights in each of the three cities, sandwiched by some effortless days in a quiet coastal hotel. The imperial cities are living showcases for some of the finest Islamic architecture in North Africa. Here severe, monumental Almohad exteriors from the 12th century can be compared with interior courtyards, decorated with all the delicacy and refinement of the Merenid 14th century.

Rabat's great era was at the end of the 12th century, when the El Hassan tower and Oudaia gate were built. The ruined necropolis of the Chellah and the medersa in neighbouring Salé are delightful survivors from the Merenid period. Rabat's shortfall is in the lack of beaches and good restaurants, but the surrounding coast makes up for this. **Casablanca** and **Témara** have celebrated restaurants while Rose Marie and Plage des Nations are secluded beach resorts.

The imperial city of Meknès was built by Moulay Ismaïl, a great if autocratic and cruel

Beat a retreat to Rabat's city gate

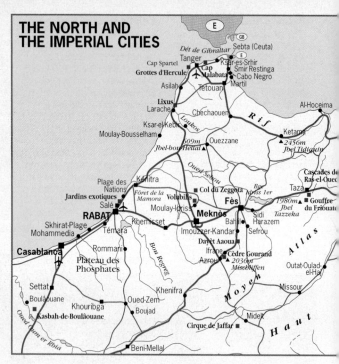

THE NORTH AND THE IMPERIAL CITIES

sultan who reigned from 1672–1727. To walk around the miles of ramparts, gates and forts here would take days. Concentrate on the principal and central sites, the souk, the intricate Bou Inania medersa, the Jamai Museum and the tomb of Moulay Ismaïl. In the later afternoon, visit the great Dar el Ma warehouse, where you can relax and enjoy the view from the rooftop garden café. The Roman ruins of **Volubilis** and the nearby pilgrimage town of **Moulay-Idriss** make a fascinating day trip from the city.

The medieval city of old Fès is the most distinctive site in Morocco. Even at its most prosaic it will provide you with unforgettable memories. Begin your visit with a scene-setting view over the old city from the Merenid tombs. There are four major sites open to the public, the Dar Batha museum, the working tanneries and the two great 14th-century Merenid medersas, Bou Inania and Attarine. Each one is overpowering in its own right, though if you are strong enough they can all be fitted into one morning. You can then spend hours, or weeks, discovering the back streets of the souk,

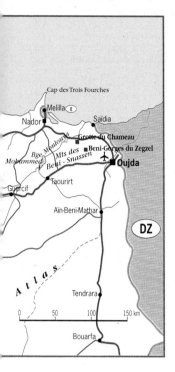

RABAT

Rabat became the modern
capital of Morocco in 1912,
during the period of French
colonial rule.
It has all the embassies, broad
avenues and public buildings
that you would expect of a
modern political centre.
However, the city is still
dominated by the Hassan tower
(Tour Hassan), its kasbah and
an enormous circuit of walls.
These are testimony of an even
greater past, when Rabat was
the 12th-century Almohad city
of Ribat el Fath, 'the citadel of
victory'.

WHAT TO SEE

◆
ALMOHAD RAMPARTS AND PALAIS ROYAL
The exterior face of the
Almohad wall from the Bab el
Had gate to Bab er Rouah is
shaded by an almost continuous
garden. The **Bab er Rouah** the
Gate of the Winds, is the only
12th-century Almohad gate to
have survived other than the
Oudaïa gate (see page 41). Its
upper rooms are occasionally
used for art exhibitions.
The **Royal Palace**, enclosed
within its own perimeter walls,
is usually open to passing traffic
and occupies the southeastern
quarter of the Almohad walled
city. There is a school, a golf
course, riding stable and
residential apartments within
the walls, but it is also at the
heart of government, with the
offices of the cabinet, council
and supreme court all housed
within the palace.

bargaining for carpets over
sweet mint tea, hunting out the
hidden residential quarters and
the reclusive courtyard
markets, and identifying the
hundreds of mosques and
tombs.
An hour's drive from Fès there
are two small and ancient
towns, **Taza** and **Sefrou**,
perched on the edge of the
Middle Atlas. The more
modern hill stations like **Ifrane**
are more popular today,
offering a quiet 'Alpine break'
off the road to Marrakech,
among the nearby forests of
cedar, lakes and a seasonal ski
run.

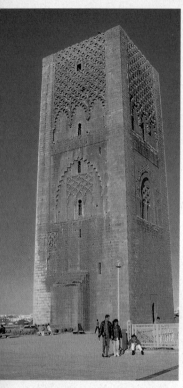

Tour Hassan, an abandoned dream

mosque, a royal cemetery and a religious college.

A guide will point out the **tomb of Shames ed Douha**, the 'Light of Dawn', who came to Morocco as a Christian slave. She became a devout Muslim and one of the wives of the black Sultan Abou Hassan, who is also buried here. Her son became the great Sultan Abou Inan, but only after he had dethroned his father.

EL HASSAN MOSQUÉE (Tour Hassan)

The minaret of the Great Mosque of El Hassan has towered above Rabat in its incomplete state since 1199. The fine stone-carved, exterior decoration serves to enhance the minaret's sense of strength. There is a ramp within, designed so that the sultan could ride to the summit and issue the call to prayer to his entire army. It was to be the final touch to the second largest mosque in the world, but work stopped the day its presiding spirit, Sultan Yaacoub el Mansour, died. After the decline of the Almohads the mosque lay neglected for centuries and was finally obliterated by an earthquake in 1755. The modern pavement and pillar bases allow you to contemplate its forbidding size.

CHELLAH

This walled necropolis housing the Merenid Sultans was built outside the Almohad city, just east of Bab Zaer gate. A pair of striking octagonal gates guards the entrance into this garden enclosure. Walk downhill past the remnants of the Roman city of **Sala Colonia** to a **sacred pool** where eels consume eggs offered to them by infertile women. Beside it rises the ruins of a 14th-century Merenid

KASBAH DES OUDAÏAS

This old Almohad fortress is named after the Oudaïa Arab tribe who formed the core of the sultans' cavalry throughout the 18th and 19th centuries.

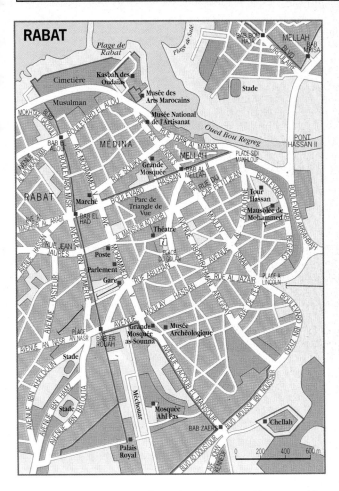

RABAT

The kasbah's most celebrated feature is its enormous 12th-century **gateway**, acknowledged to be a masterpiece of Islamic design, subtly combining form and decoration. Gates had more than just a defensive function in Muslim society, for they also served as an accepted political forum where petitioners would wait and justice would be seen to be administered. The kasbah's walls are mighty – 10 feet (3m) thick and 30 feet (10m) high. Originating in the 12th century, they were repeatedly reinforced throughout history. The kasbah is no longer the seat of government, and is filled by a village of whitewashed houses typical of Andalucia. From the terrace there is a fine view over the **Bou Regreg estuary**, which once sheltered a formidable fleet of pirate ships. Below it the 18th-century coastal batteries were installed to defend this safe anchorage from European bombardment – the last of which was launched by the Austrian navy in 1829. Tucked away below the batteries and just above the small town beach is a licensed restaurant, **La Caravelle**.

◆
MAUSOLÉE DU MOHAMMED V
To the south of the Great Mosque of El Hassan stands the mausoleum of Mohammed V and a library and mosque dedicated to his memory. The father of the present king, he remains a great national hero, having led his people in the fight for independence. No expense has been spared in creating this lavish white tomb chamber, and its dazzling interior is almost overpoweringly rich. As well as the pomp of the scarlet-clad guards and heraldic banner, however, there is a quiet Islamic dignity. A tomb of white Afghan onyx lies on a mirror-like floor of black marble.

◆
MÉDINA
This old quarter of Rabat was established in the early 17th century by Muslims from Spain,

bringing new life to the Almohad city which had lain empty for centuries. The old 12th-century ramparts enclosed an enormous area, so the settlers constructed an interior wall, along present day avenue Hassan II. The gates which pierce this Andalucian wall give entrance to the main vegetable market and thoroughfares of the souk. Rue des Consuls is the smartest alley, filled with carpet bazaars which woo the tourists, echoing the time in the 18th century when the area was set aside for European merchants and consuls. It leads out into an open area known as Souk el Ghezel, the wool market.

◆◆
MUSÉE ARCHÉOLOGIE (Archaeological Museum)
rue al Brihi
This small but rewarding museum is tucked away in the back streets beside the Great Mosque (Grande Mosquée), at the head of avenue Mohammed V. The main hall displays finds from Sala Colonia, the Roman city at Ribat. The adjacent **Hall of Bronzes** houses magnificent busts of Cato and King Juba II, discovered at Volubilis. There is also a full length bronze copy of Praxiteles' crowned Ephebus and sculptures of a dog, a fisherman and a legless rider among other assorted treasures.
Open: 08.30–12.00 and 14.30–18.00 hrs. (June to September 09.00–15.00 hrs.) Closed Tuesday.

Mausolée du Mohammed V, Rabat

◆◆
MUSÉE DES ARTS MAROCAINS (National Museum of Moroccan Crafts)

A museum of national crafts occupies an intimate 17th-century palace built by Sultan Moulay Ismaïl in the lower kasbah. It houses a dusty but absorbing collection of traditional ceramics, costume, killims, carpets, musical instruments and armour. These are housed in various dark halls, pavilions and elegant reception rooms surrounding the central Moorish garden. To complete the attractions there is the **Café Maure**.

Museum open: 08.30–12.00 and 14.30–18.00 hrs, (June to September 09.00–15.00 hrs.) Closed Tuesdays.

Accommodation
Expensive

The Safir and La Tour Hassan hotels are two luxurious, 'international' hotels in the centre of town. The **Safir** is on place Sidi Makhlouf (tel: (07) 732117), the five-star **La Tour Hassan** at 34 avenue Abderrahmane Annegay (tel: (07) 733815).

Moderate
Hotel Chellah, 2 rue d'Ifni (tel: (07) 765454) is less glitzy but efficient and comfortable. Four stars.

Going slightly downmarket try **Hotel Balima** (tel: (07) 707755) which has an imposing exterior, a popular café and is directly opposite the parliament on avenue Mohammed V. Three stars.

Restaurants

Rabat's restaurants are comparatively dull and you will be better off eating in the major hotels here.

The **Diffa Restaurant** in La Tour Hassan is the best and can be relied upon for a feast, as can the traditional Moroccan restaurant in the Safir. Otherwise, drive out to Témara (see **Beach Resorts below**).

Nightlife

There are bars and nightclubs with floor shows in **Hotel La Tour Hassan** and in the **Hyatt Regency** (tel: (07) 771234) on the southern edge of the city.

Shopping

Rabat is the traditional Moroccan source of carpets in the prayer mat design, which borrowed certain motifs from Persia. Have a look in the **National Craft Museum** and the showroom on rue Tarik al Marsa (open: daily 09.00–12.00 and 15.00–18.00 hrs) before browsing in the bazaars along rue des Consuls.

The other medina streets stock a good range of hats and embroidered accessories.

WHAT TO SEE AROUND RABAT

◆

BEACH RESORTS

North of Rabat stretches **Plage des Nations**, a sandy beach favoured by the diplomatic community, with just one hotel,

the elegant **Hotel Firdaous** (tel: (07) 738332).

Immediately south of the city is **Témara**, whose greatest attraction is a modern, well-stocked zoo and two fine restaurants, one in the beachfront **La Felouque Hotel** (expensive), the other the mid-town **Restaurant Provençal**. Some nine miles (15km) beyond Témara, **Rose Marie Plage**, also known as Ech-Chiahna, has a much better beach, shared between a campsite and the swish four-star **Club Hotel La Kasbah** (tel: (07) 749133).

The three-star **Hotel Amphitrite** (tel: (07) 742236), at **Skhirat** beyond, is a smaller, tranquil and expensive hotel beside the royal beach palace. Still further south, **Mohammedia** is a more lively resort equipped with two nightclubs (the **Fedala** and the **Sphinx**), a golf course, a race track and a small, old town which shelters behind the low walls of a 16th-century Portuguese fort. Stay in either of the town's two smart hotels, the five-star **Miramar** (tel: (03) 322021) or the three-star **Samir** (tel: (03) 310770).

◆

CASABLANCA

57 miles (92km) south of Rabat

Thousands of visitors, reared on the romantic images of *Casablanca* the movie, are sorely disappointed by Casablanca the city. The film was shot entirely in Hollywood in 1942 and made no attempt to portray the real place. There is no Sam's Bar here, and no

Aspiring modernity in Casablanca

Dooley Wilson singing 'As Time Goes By'. Nor does the expanding industrial city boast much of indigenous cultural interest and there is not a single museum or ancient monument to be seen.

If you cannot resist visiting, a day here might begin with a drink in the lobby of the glittering Hyatt Regency hotel on place Mohammed V. Strolling up the busy central street of the old medina, you reach an 18th-century artillery bastion, **La Sqala**, with a view over the old port.

The French-built new medina (1 mile/1.5km southeast of the old town) contains mosques, gardens, a royal palace and arcaded streets. It is the most elegant part of town and contains the most hassle-free market in Morocco.

The city tour concludes with a drive along the coast road, past the enormous Great Mosque, to the lighthouse on the El Hank peninsula, where there are a couple of elegant fish restaurants such as **Le Cabestan** (tel: (02) 391190), and **La Mer** (tel: (02) 363315).

Accommodation
Casablanca is a city of businessmen not tourists, so if you do stay here there is a good choice of luxury hotels. Smartest is the de luxe five-star **Hyatt Regency** on place Mohammed V (tel: (02) 261234) with the **Hotel Safir** at 160 avenue des FAR (tel: (02) 311212) and the **El Mansour** at 27 avenue des FAR (tel: (02) 313011) – both five stars – not far behind. Somewhat cheaper is the old-fashioned two-star **Hotel Excelsior** at 2 rue Nolly (tel: (02) 200263).

◆
JARDINS EXOTIQUES
(Bouknadel Gardens)
7 miles (12km) northeast of Rabat

M François, a French ecologist, poet and botanist, created this spectacular series of gardens in the 1950s on a thin belt of sandy coastal land. A number of colour-coded paths take the visitor past bridges and decaying follies. The first garden contains a collection of plants indigenous to Morocco, the second recreates a traditional formal Moorish garden. The third is even more ambitious, aiming at a recreation of the flora of America, Asia, the Pacific, Indo-China and the West Indies. There are signed routes you can follow.

Open: 09.00–18.30 hrs.

◆◆
SALÉ
On the opposite bank of the Bou Regreg, Rabat's river, is a separate walled city, called Salé. It feels almost rural in comparison with its big brother, but from the 13th to the 18th centuries, Salé was the dominant partner. It was the infamous base of the Salé Rovers, Muslim pirates who plundered the Atlantic trade routes and raided for slaves as far north as Iceland.

The massive 13th-century **Bab Mrisa**, once a watergate, is now landlocked. It used to guard the entrance to the city's dockyards. The smaller gate beside it, the **Bab Mellah**, was the entrance to the Jewish quarter. Nowadays it is bus-cluttered **Bab Fès** that marks the principal entrance into the old town.

You will need a guide to navigate you through the medina souks to reach the 14th-century Merenid **Medersa**. This now-empty residential college for Koranic studies was built by the black sultan, Abou Hassan, who is buried in Rabat. It has a covered prayer hall and a small open courtyard where the traditional decoration of coloured tiles, carved plaster and cedar seems all the more dazzling. There are two galleries of boarding rooms above and a rooftop view over the medina.

MEKNÈS

Though Meknès was once the capital of Morocco, and abounds with buildings from the city's heyday, today the city has a somewhat provincial air. Its markets groan under the produce of the rich surrounding agricultural land, but for the visitor it is the walled medina and the old imperial quarter that fascinate. When Sultan Moulay Ismaïl came to the throne in 1672, he turned his back on the turbulent citizens of Fès and Marrakech, and built a new capital here, where he had served as the town's governor

Flying saucers in a Meknès souk

during the reign of his elder brother. Throughout his long reign (to 1727) tens of thousands of slaves were continuously employed in the construction of the new imperial city. It grew into a vast walled enclosure of hidden palaces, storerooms and pavilions, with barracks housing an army of 25,000 Negro slaves.

WHAT TO SEE

BAB MANSOUR EL ALEUJ
This massive gate, decorated with Roman columns from Volubilis, was one of the original entrances to the

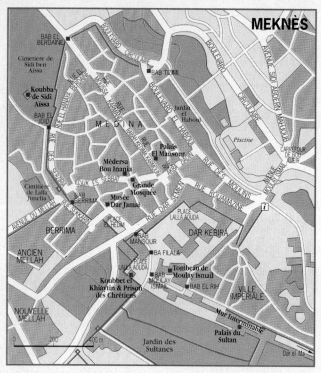

MEKNÈS

17th-century imperial city. Its
north face looks out across the
medina's imposing place El
Hedim, where a line of mosaic-
tiled fountains play fitfully. The
south face overlooks the quieter
place Lalla Aouda, once
bordered by 25 separate
palaces. The gate is named
after El Aleuj, Sultan Moulay
Ismaïl's architect, who was a
Christian convert to Islam. It
functions as a central landmark
in the city but is in fact
somewhat squat and heavy. El
Aleuj created a number of more
elegant gates, including the
neighbouring **Bab En Nour**.

◆◆◆
DAR EL MA
Imperial city
A one-mile (2km) drive
between a double skin of walls
takes you from the Bab
Mansour to the Dar el Ma which
is also known as the Heri es
Souani. It is an enormous,
vaulted warehouse built by
Moulay Ismaïl to safeguard the
stores for his army. The roof of
its cavernous silos still supports
a miraculous café set among an
orchard of olive trees. From this
vantage point you can see over
other features of the old
imperial city. Immediately

beside it are the pillars of another granary and to the west is the **Aguedal**, an immense royal water reservoir. Today, in what used to be mere paddocks for the sultan's horses, stand a campsite, a race course, a horticultural garden and Morocco's Dar el Beida military academy. Beyond, you can just make out the ruins of the **Heri el Mansour**, the stables, which once held more than 12,000 horses.
Open: 07.00–12.30 and 15.00–18.00 hrs.

Ruined granary in Meknès

◆◆
KOUBBET EL KHIAYTIN and PRISON DES CHRÉTIENS
Imperial city
From place Lalla Aouda pass under the Filala arch to reach the Koubbet el Khiyatin tucked in the corner of a garden square. This small kiosk with its carved Koranic script was used by Sultan Moulay Ismaïl for the reception of foreign

embassies. Beside it is the entrance to a massive underground network of storerooms, which has become an apocryphal 'Christian Prison', supposedly for Christian slaves.
Open: 08.00–12.00 and 14.30–18.00 hrs.
In the other corner of the square, a guarded gateway gives entrance to the Royal Golf Club, landscaped within the old palace garden.

◆◆◆
MÉDERSA BOU INANIA
Medina
This elegant medersa was completed during the reign of the Merenid Sultan Abou Inan, 1351–58. It follows the classic plan for a residential college, most splendidly represented in **Fès** (see page 54). A domed hall leads into the confined space of an open-air courtyard, with a marble pavement and central pool. A gallery runs around three faces supporting two storeys of bedrooms, while the fourth side is filled by a cool and elegant prayer hall. This, as well as the hall of the nearby Great Mosque (Grande Mosquée), was used for lectures and readings where the *tolba*, the students, studied the Koran and its related legal codes. All the layers of decoration, the cut tile, carved plaster and cedar, are bound together by bands of Koranic script, just as the Muslim world is held together by the words of God.
Open: Monday to Thursday 09.00–12.00 and 15.00–18.00 hrs (July to September 09.00–17.00).

MUSÉE DAR JAMAI
Medina

This 19th-century vizier's palace, with its small but delightful garden, houses a collection of traditional arts and crafts. The architectural fittings of the palace are the perfect complement to the display of jewellery, ceramics, killims and ironwork. Do not miss the furnished reception room upstairs, the splendidly complex keys or the silk banner of Sultan Moulay Hassan.
Open: Monday to Friday 09.00–12.00 and 15.00–18.00 hrs (July to September 09.00–17.00 hrs).

SOUK
Medina

The heart of the souk is in the confusing web of streets around the Great Mosque (Grande Mosquée), recognisable by its five elaborately decorated gates. Hire a guide to take you to the bazaars, like **El Mansour**, which are housed in elegant Moorish palaces.

◆◆
TOMBEAU DE MOULAY ISMAÏL (Tomb Mosque of Moulay Ismaïl)
Imperial city

A visitor passes through three great tiled courtyards before arriving at the fountain court. Here Moroccan visitors stop to pray and tourists also respectfully remove their shoes before advancing into the ornate Moorish hall where you can look on to the marble tomb of the sultan. He was a great correspondent, and among other concerns of state advised James II to become a Muslim and proposed marriage to one of Louis XIV's daughters. The clocks beside the tomb are supposedly part of the gifts that accompanied a polite refusal.
Open: Monday to Thursday 08.00–13.00 and 15.00–19.00 hrs (July to September 09.00–17.00 hrs).

Accommodation

Hotel Rif on rue d'Accra (tel: (05) 522591) is a comfortable hotel whose bar, nightclub and restaurants function as a smart social centre for the French-built new town.

Probably the best of Meknès' hotels is the **Transatlantique** on rue el Meriniyine (tel: (05) 525050) which has a superb view over the medina. There are also a number of good cheap hotels along avenue des FAR – the one-star **Panorama** (tel: (05) 522737), the **Continental** (tel: (05) 525471), the **Excelsior** (tel: (05) 521900) and three-star **Hotel Volubilis** (tel: (05) 520102).

Restaurants

Meknès is no gourmet's paradise, but the **Zitouna Restaurant** (tel: (05) 530281), set in a medina town house, is fun at lunchtime, and for dinner you can choose between the restaurants in the Rif and the Transatlantique hotels.

Festivals

September is Meknès' busy month, with a **Fantasia Festival** followed by *moussems* at nearby Moulay-Idriss and Sidi Bouzelm.

FÈS

Dyed skins drying outside Fès

Fès el Bali, the old city, is the best preserved medieval Muslim city in the world. It is an astonishing and confusing place where elegance and squalor mingle freely. The air is filled with conflicting smells and sounds, its packed warren-like streets clear only at the cry of 'balak', the warning shout of working muleteers.

Fès has served as the cultural and mercantile centre of Morocco since its foundation by Moulay Idriss in 799. The three centuries of Merenid rule, from the capture of the city by the Beni Merin tribe in 1248 to 1541 (when the Saadians occupied Fès), were the golden period of its history. Even then the Fassi, the citizens of Fès, were far from complacent and quick to revolt.

The Merenid sultans never lived in the old city, but ruled instead from the royal palace inside **Fès Jdid**, a separate and defendable city which they built to the west. The odd shape of the city was further exaggerated when the French built a new town still further west.

Official guides can be arranged by your hotel or hired from the Tourist Office on place de la Résistance in the new town, from the Syndicat d'Initiative on place Mohammed V, or can be picked up at Bab Bou Jeloud, the entrance to the medina:

WHAT TO SEE

◆◆◆
FÈS EL BALI

The Talaa Kebira and Talaa Seghira are the two principal alleyways running from Bab Bou Jeloud through the heart of the medina. Narrow alleys lead off the quiet residential quarters or expose a secretive baker's oven, a hammam furnace, a line of grill cafés, a busy workshop or one of the river-powered mills.

Your guide will also show you some of the acknowledged highlights, which include

Brazen glory; the royal palace gates

tambourine manufacturers in the skinners' fondouk, leather workers in Souk Ain Allou, the tree-shaded Souk el Henna, the dyers' souk, metalworkers in the place Seffarine and the Nejjarine fountain.

The **Kissaria** is the densest area of the medina,

surrounding the holy tomb of Moulay Idriss II. This, like the nearby Great Mosque of Qaraouiyne, is inaccessible to non-Muslims. Two opulent neighbouring bazaars, Fondouk Tsetaouine and Palais de Fès, have views into the Great Mosque from their roof terraces however.

For many visitors, the rooftop view over the open-air tannery above the River Fès provides the most memorable experience in Fès. The unpleasant odour – a sore trial for the squeamish – is compensated for by the array of startling coloured vats and drying skins, and by the skill and labour of the workmen.

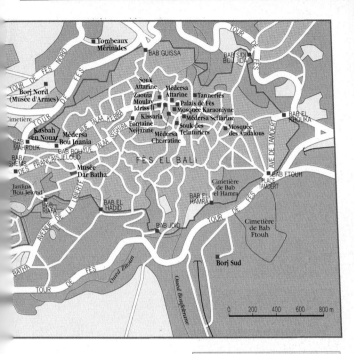

♦
FÈS JDID

Place des Alaouites is a vast open space, the formal approach to the gleaming brass gates of the royal palace. From here grande rue des Mérinides passes through the **mellah**, the old Jewish ghetto, with its distinctive first-floor balconies, narow side alleys and jewellery shops. Bab Semmarin marks the entrance into Fès Jdid proper. Pass through the triple-bayed Bab Dekakène, to enter the old Mechouar square. Avenue des Français leads east, alongside the Bou Jeloud public gardens and towards the striking Bou Jeloud arch.

♦♦♦
MÉDERSA ATTARINE ✓

Fès el Bali
This is the finest of the half dozen medersas that cluster round the periphery of the Great Mosque of Qaraouiyne. The medersa was built in the early 14th century by Sultan Abou Said. It is a gem of Hispano-Mauresque architecture, the lavish decoration conspiring to create a tranquil, reflective space without overwhelming the small courtyard and prayer hall. It has 60 bedrooms where students lodged.
Open: 09.00–12.00 and 14.00–18.00hrs. Closed Friday mornings.

◆◆◆ MÉDERSA BOU INANIA ✓

Fès el Bali

This, the grandest of all the Merenid medersas, was built in the mid-14th century by Sultan Abou Inan. When faced with the bill the sultan declared, 'What is enthralling is never too costly' – but he was only speaking half the truth. He also hoped that his new medersa would diminish the influence of the university of Qaraouiyne – established in Fès long before the first European university – and for this he was willing to pay dearly. Before entering the medersa, look high up on the street opposite and you will see the row of windows and brass bowls of the medersa's once-famous water clock. The open central courtyard with its round pool is flanked by two lecture rooms and a prayer hall which is inaccessible to non-Muslims as it remains in active use. In the floor above, the rooms of the students are arranged. The building is in the style perfected by the Moors in Andalucia, with elaborate decoration in mosaic, plaster and cedar as expression of divine symmetry.

Open: 08.00–19.00 hrs. Closed Friday mornings.

Looking good enough to eat: some of Fès' palaces are now restaurants

MUSÉE DAR BATHA

The palace of Dar Batha was
built by the 19th-century Sultan
Moulay Hassan in the wasteland
between Fès Jdid and Fès el
Bali. Its red walls hide an
elegant Moorish garden, and
the audience chambers now
house a collection of traditional
arts. Astrolabes mingle with
illuminated Korans, rough
Berber jewellery with the
elegant blue and white
ceramics of Fès.
Open: 09.00–12.00 and
15.00–18.00 hrs. Closed
Tuesdays.

TOMBEAUX MÉRINIDES
(Merenid Tombs)

On the high ground to the north
of Fès el Bali the scant ruins of
the Merenids' tombs make a
spectacular viewing platform
over the old city.
Taking a taxi up here from the
new town, you pass the long
outer walls of the royal palace
and turn uphill by Bab Segma
with its striking 14th-century
octagonal tower. Above is the
17th-century walled Kasbah des
Cherada, which now houses a
hospital and university and is
not open to the public.
The 16th-century artillery
fortress of **Borj Nord** is now a
weaponry museum.
Open: 08.30–12.00 and
14.30–18.00. Closed
Tuesdays.
Looking out across the mass of
the old city from the Merenid
tombs, the tomb of Moulay
Idriss II can be recognised
beneath its striking green
pyramid roof, to the right of the
Great Mosque of Qaraouiyne
and its two minarets.

Accommodation
Expensive

Hotel de Fès on avenue des
FAR (tel: (05) 625002) is the
most lavish and efficient of Fès's
hotels. Five stars.
The **Palais Jamai** at Bab Guissa
in the old city (tel: (05) 634331),
on the other hand, is a firm
favourite with many visitors.
Established in 1930 in a 19th-
century vizier's palace, it has an
elegant, time-worn cachet and
literary associations. It has a
hammam of its own and an
excellent view of the medina.
Five stars.

Moderate

Try either the hotel **De la Paix**
in avenue Hassan II (tel: (05)
625072) which has rooms with
en suite bathrooms and is very
clean or the **Moissafir** at
avenue des Almohades
(tel: (05) 651902).

Restaurants

Within the old city a number of
merchants' palaces have been
turned into distinctive
restaurants. For lunch ask your
guide to take you to either the
Dar Tajine (tel: (05) 634167),
the **Palais des Mérénides**
(tel: (05) 634028) or the **Palais
M'Nebhi** (tel: (05) 633893).
For a lively dinner with a floor
show a taxi can take you close
to the **Restaurant Firdaous**
(tel: (05) 634343) by Bab
Guissa. Distinguished cooking
can be had in the restaurants in
the Hotel de Fès, Hotel les
Mérénides and the Palais
Jamai.

WHAT TO SEE AROUND MEKNÈS AND FÈS

◆

IMOUZZER-KANDAR, IFRANE and AZROU

around 30 miles (50km) south of Fés

These three small hill-towns are popular resorts in the muggy summer months. Surrounded by forests, orchards, lakes and mountains, they have a second season, as skiing resorts, when there is snow on Mount Mischliffen in winter. The clumps of Atlas cedar scattered among alpine meadows near the mountain are magnificent.

Imouzzer-Kandar is locally esteemed for its apple orchards and a three-day 'fête des pommes' (apple festival) in July.

Ifrane, with its hilltop modern royal palace, immaculate colonial villas and glitzy riverside gardens, is the smartest resort.

Azrou, equidistant from Fès and Meknès, is the busiest and least affected. A track just outside Azrou signposted to the **Cèdre Gourand** (Gourand Cedar), twists through three miles (5km) of dense woodland on its way to admire the enormous girth of this tree, which was named after the second French colonial governor of Morocco.

Dayèt (Lake) Aaoua is the largest lake in the area, just off the main Imouzzer–Ifrane road. From here a signposted system of dirt tracks takes in a beautiful series of local lakes and valleys. Other lesser attractions include the Tuesday market at Azrou and the gurgling banks of the River Tizguit in Ifrane.

Accommodation

Ifrane has all the best hotels in the region. The glittering, hilltop **Hotel Mischliffen** (tel: (05) 566607) is filled with courtiers when the king is in residence. Five-stars.

The mock-Alpine **Grand Hotel** on avenue de la Marche Verte (tel: (05) 566203) is comfortable and well-run. Two stars.

Overlooking the shore of Dayèt Aaoua, the **Chalet du Lac** (tel: 0 – through the Azrou post office) is a serene and peaceful choice for a stay. There are also half a dozen small hotels and pensions in Azrou and Imouzzer, in addition to campsites and youth hostels.

◆

MIDELT

119 miles (192km) southeast of Meknès

This unpretentious highland town is a useful and cool stop-over for those taking the direct road from Fès to the far south. There is a small killim market in the central Souk el Jdid, some roadside restaurants and a hotel, the three-star **Ayachi** (tel: (05) 582161), in a comfortable colonial chalet on the southern edge of town. The staff in the Ayachi organise a 'Cirque du Jaffar', a landrover tour through the forested foothills of the nearby Middle Atlas peaks. You can walk to some nearby ksar villages.

MOULAY-IDRISS
15 miles (24km) north of Meknès
Moulay Idriss, a kinsman of the Prophet Mohammed, established the first independent Muslim kingdom in this area in the 8th century. His **tomb**, in the centre of the town which bears his name, was miraculously rediscovered in the 15th century and quickly became the centre of a celebrated national pilgrimage and festival. Five visits to Moulay-Idriss were widely considered to be equivalent to the pilgrimage to Mecca, one of the obligations of the Muslim faith. The festival is still enormously popular and is held in the presence of the king every September.

The mosque and outbuildings which surround the tomb are marked off by a wooden barrier and are strictly forbidden to non-Muslims. Tourists are welcome to wander around the central market and the picturesque back streets of this holy town, unevenly draped over twin hills. No hotels have been allowed but there is a delightful, unlicensed, roadside restaurant, the **Baraka de Zerhoun**, at 22 Ain Smen Khiber (tel: (05) 544184).

SEFROU
17 miles (28km) southeast of Fès
This ancient market town, perched on the foothills of the Middle Atlas, once benefited from its position on the old trading route to the Sahara. It was celebrated for its large Jewish community and its claim to have been the first capital of Moulay Idriss in the 8th century, but is now more famous for its cherry harvest. The old quarter is like a miniature Fès, with a complete circuit of ramparts enclosing a cramped town strung along both banks of a mountain stream. There is a craft centre and garden just beside place Moulay Hassan, whence two gates, Bab Taksebt and Bab Mkam, mark the start of the medina. Outside the town you can visit the Oued Aggai waterfall, the hilltop shrine of Sidi Bou Ali and the pretty nearby village of Bahlil.

Accommodation
The **Sidi Lahcen Lysoussi** hotel (tel: (05) 660497), uphill from the post office in the new town, has a bar, a restaurant and a small garden. Two stars.

TAZA
75 miles (120km) east of Fès
The ancient citadel of Taza guards the eastern approaches to central Morocco. Its strategic position has given it a violent history but not without a brief period of glory, when it served as the Almohad capital in the 12th century. Taza was the first city to fall to the Merenids in the 13th century. The old town sits on a natural rock fortress, commanding the narrow valley that separates the Rif from the Middle Atlas mountains. Its surrounding

walls are pierced by half a dozen gates and reinforced with bastions. Two most distinctive features are **El Sarassine**, a 12th-century round tower, and **El Bastioun**, a 16th-century brick blockhouse. Meander west from place Moulay Hassan to find the alleys of the souk and the thoroughfare that runs straight through the heart of the old town. At the southern end of town it terminates at the elegant Mechouar square before the **Andalucian Mosque**, and at the northern end in front of the Almohad **Grand Mosque**. Wind your way past its venerable and inaccessible (to non-Muslims) 12th-century prayer hall to reach **Bab er Rih**, the gate of winds, which has a fine view out over olive groves and gardens.

The Jbel Tazzeka range of the Middle Atlas mountains rise immediately south of town. The cork woods and café round the usually dry **Ras Waterfall** give a fine view over Taza. Climb on up the pass of Sidi Mejbeur to alpine pasture and a pair of seasonal lakes. From here a track leads up to **Friouato Cavern** (Gouffre du Friouato), 590 feet (180m) deep, which despite its natural skylight requires a torch as you descend.

Accommodation

The **Friouato Hotel** (tel: (05) 672593) is hidden away in the olive grove that still separates the regular avenues of Taza new town from the old citadel. Three stars.

◆◆◆
VOLUBILIS ✓

3 miles (5km) from Moulay-Idriss

The Roman ruins at Volubilis are the most important and impressive in Morocco. This city was the western capital of the North African King Juba II before the Romans annexed his kingdom in AD44. It then served as a Roman provincial capital for 250 years before it was sacked by the native Baquates tribe at the end of the 3rd century.

The first stop in the established itinerary round this hilltop site is at an **olive press**, one of many in the city, complete with a millstone, press footings and separation tanks (the process is vividly revealed by a restored press which has recently been added to the site). The nearby **House of Orpheus** is named after the mosaic found in the dining-room, which shows the bard surrounded by an audience of animals.

Ahead, the paved **forum**, centre of civic life in the city, is still dominated by the arched outside wall of the law courts, the **Basilica**. Standing Corinthian colums belong to the **Capitoline temple** which originally would have been enclosed within its own arcaded courtyard. It was dedicated to the official cult of Jupiter, Juno and Minerva. Before reaching the magnificent **Triumphal Arch**, you pass the **House of the Athlete** with its simple mosaic and, on the other side of the Roman road, the ruins of a large public

The ruins of the city of Volubilis

bathhouse. The arch was restored by French archaeologists, having been ruined in the great earthquake of 1755. It was built to honour the Severan dynasty of emperors who came from North Africa. From the arch runs the broad avenue, **Decumanus Maximus**, at the far end of which the Tingis (Tanger) Gate once stood. To the south and east a ring of Roman forts protected the city. In its heyday, Decumanus Maximus avenue was lined by shops. Behind them stood the smartest city houses, now named after the mosaics found within. At the far end of the avenue, a dozen Ionic columns heralds the **Gordian palace**, seat of the governor. As a suitable finale, head for the **House of Venus**, marked out by a single cypress tree. Here there are three delightful mosaics: one of a bird-powered chariot race; another of Hylos, the boyfriend of Hercules, being abducted by nymphs; and a portrayal of Diana, the virgin and vengeful goddess of hunting, being surprised while bathing by Actaeon.
Open: daily sunrise–sunset.

MARRAKECH AND THE HIGH ATLAS

The red-walled city of Marrakech with its great souk, ancient monuments and blue backdrop of mountains is one of the world's most distinctive cities. It sits at the centre of a region where the Mediterranean and Saharan cultures and climates meet. Marrackech's central square, the **Jemaa el Fna**, reflects this dual pulse with its conflicting strains of music. Here the

MARRAKECH AND THE SOUTH

haunting melodies picked out on wailing Saharan clarinets swirl among the saccharine Arabic love songs of Egypt and Syria. When in Marrakech it is helpful to take a historical overview to clarify the monuments. Scan back over the centuries to the desert-born Almoravides who first created the city in the 11th century. They live still through their long ramparts and the pavilion known as the **Koubba el Baraoudiyn**, a lone testimony to the elegant city which was

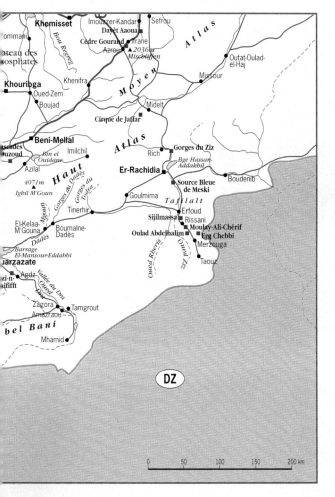

completely destroyed in 1147.
Marrakech was then entirely
recreated by the Almohads
whose great **Koutoubia** minaret
still dominates the skyline. The
Saadian sultans restored the
city in the 16th century and
have left the magnificent **Ben
Youssef medersa**, the
extraordinary interiors of the
Saadian tombs and the ruined
mass of the **El Badia palace**.
The **Dar Si Said** and **Bahia**
palaces on the other hand were
not finished until the turn of the
century.

You should try to make time for
a trip to at least one of the old
Atlantic ports that served
Marrakech. Choose between
El-Jadida with its bastions, long
beach and Portuguese cistern,
Oualidia, which overlooks a
lagoon, **Safi**, famous for its
potters, sardines and castles
and **Essaouira**, home of wind,
18th-century walls and
woodcarvers.

The magnificent High Atlas
mountains conceal a number of
jewels within their folds
including thundering **Ouzoud
waterfall** (Cascade d'Ouzoud),
the steep-sided **Ourika valley**
with its market and restaurants,
Jbel Toubkal, the highest
mountain in North Africa and
the dizzy mountain road that
crosses the mountains at the
Tizi-n-Test pass. Man-made
sites and amusements include
the ski resort at **Oukaïmeden**,
the ruined palace of **Telouet**,
perched just off the Tizi-n-
Tichka pass and the 12th-
century Almohad shrine,
Tin-Mal Mosque, on the Tizi-n-
Test.

Charm rises to the occasion

MARRAKECH

The red walls, monuments and extensive markets of Marrakech, overlooked by the celebrated Koutoubia minaret, make this city the most popular destination in Morocco. An almost Himalayan backdrop provided by the High Atlas mountains, and the modern conveniences of an international airport, car rental firms and dozens of luxurious hotels are icing on the cake. Staying in Marrakech is an asault on the senses which sometimes threatens to overpower, but with a map from the tourist office and the help of a local guide the city offers several days' entrancing exploration.

Marrakech's real fascination has deep roots, for it is a living expression of the marriage between Islam and the native Berbers of Africa. It was founded around the turn of the 11th century as a forward base for the Almoravides, Berber nomads from the Western Sahara who were fired by a burning desire to reform Islam. They were the first dynasty to unite the whole country, and Marrakech was later transformed into a true city by skilled Andalucian craftsmen employed after the conquest of Spain. The city went on to become the capital of the even more militant and powerful Almohad Empire, and was restored from near ruin by the 16th-century Saadian dynasty. Until the arrival of the French, it functioned, with Fès, as the dual capital of Morocco.

WHAT TO SEE

BAB AGUENAOU
medina – south
This magnificent gate, with its wide, stone-carved, sunburst arch, was the principal entrance to the Almohad kasbah. Once a vulnerable corner of the fortified city, this area was later reinforced by the nearby, squat **Bab er Rob**, now the focus of a pottery and vegetable market.

DAR SI SAÏD
medina – east
This older but more modest palace was occupied by the family that built the **Bahia** (see page 67). It provides a delightful backdrop for a collection of traditional arts and crafts. This includes some fine pieces of 16th-century carving from the El Badia palace, a good collection of embroidery and costumes and some interesting examples of local 19th-century carpets. In addition there are displays of kitchenware, arms and Berber jewellery.
Open: 09.00–12.00 and 14.30–18.00 hrs. Closed Tuesdays. From July to September 09.00–12.00 and 16.00–19.00 hrs.

EL BADIA
medina – south
Ahmed el Mansour built El Badia, 'the incomparable', as a fitting consummation of his glorious reign. Only the

towering earth walls now
remain, but these bare bones,
surrounding four sunken
gardens, a vast reception hall,
side pavilions and pools, allow
one to imagine the grandeur of
this once-glittering edifice.
Pass through a gate in the
southeast to explore the old
cellars and kitchen area. The
feasts that marked the
opening of El Badia in 1603
were of unparalleled
magnificence. During a gap in
the festivities, the old sultan
turned to his fool for praise.
This prescient and audacious
courtier replied that the palace
would make a fine ruin. Within a
hundred days Ahmed was dead
and before the end of the
century his palace was totally
gutted.
Open: daily 08.30–18.00 hrs.

◆

JARDIN MAJORELLE
*new town, off avenue Yacoub
el Mansour*
This famous walled garden was
created by Jaques and Louis
Majorelle (father and son
Orientalist artists) and is now
maintained by Yves St Laurent,
the famous North African born
fashion designer, whose
collection is displayed in a
small four-room museum
(separate admission) within the
gardens.
Its collection of cacti, blue-
painted pavilions, pools and
watercourses have been used
in countless fashion shots.
Open: daily 08.00–12.00 and
14.00–17.00 hrs. (July to
September 08.00–12.00 and
15.00–19.00 hrs). *No children
admitted.*

◆◆◆ JEMAA EL FNA ✓

medina – centre
The name of the central square
in Marrakech morbidly
translates as the 'place of the

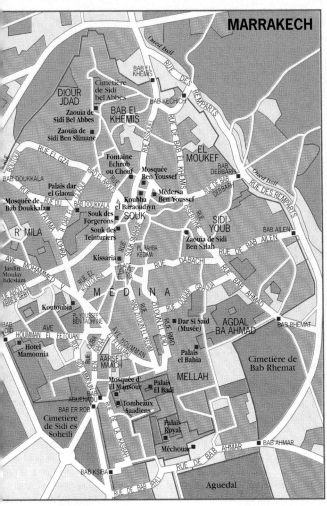

MARRAKECH

dead'. In fact it is one of the most lively and famous public squares in the world, devoid of architectural interest but packed full of human activity. The barrows of orange-juice squeezers and nut salesmen form a rough cordon within which musicians, dancers, magicians, snake-charmers and storytellers perform for a mixed audience of tourists, farmers and Marrakechis. At dusk the throng is further complicated by

Dancing in the streets of Marrakech

lines of smoking grill and fry restaurants, impromptu street markets, beggars and touts. It is an exhilarating but exhausting daily spectacle. You can have your fortune told, listen to native music and try the variety of local food on sale. Stock up on loose change and smiles, and recover over a glass of mint tea on one of the terraces of the cafés that overlook the square.

◆

KOUBBA EL BARAOUDIYN

medina – north

Hidden behind a dusty wall beside the Ben Youssef mosque sits the only surviving structure from 11th-century Almoravide Marrakech. This small pavilion, used originally for washing before prayers, may not look much from the outside but stare up into the dome and you will understand some of the

excitement it stirs in experts. You are looking at the earliest example of Moorish carving in North Africa. From this seed blossomed the rich decorative tradition known as Hispano-Mauresque, which dominates North African art and architecture to this day.
Open: daily 08.00–12.00 and 14.30–18.00 hrs.

◆◆◆

MÉDERSA BEN YOUSSEF

medina – north

The 16th-century Ben Youssef medersa is the largest medersa in the country, grander than the earlier and more intricate Merenid colleges. It was designed as a residential college for students, who lodged at the medersa while they memorised the Koran and studied commentaries and religious law in the cool prayer hall of the nearby mosque of Ben Youssef.

The large open courtyard is a riot of decoration, using chipped-tile mosaic, carved plaster and cedar, knitted together by lines of Koranic script. It is framed by flanking galleries and centres on a pool which points directly at the elaborate mihrab niche in the prayer hall. Upstairs the monastic cells of the students are open to examination.

The Ben Youssef medersa was built in less than a year on the orders of Abdullah el Ghalib, a great Saadian sultan who reigned from 1557–1574. The Saadians loathed Fès and planned to break its intellectual monopoly by building this college.

Open: 08.00–12.00 and 14.30–18.00 hrs. Closed Monday and Friday mornings.

◆◆
MOSQUÉE KOUTOUBIA
south of avenue Mohammed V
The minaret of the Koutoubia mosque towers over the city. Each of its façades is decorated with a different carved ornamentation, creating a valuable blueprint of Almohad design. It was finished in the last years of the 12th century, when an empire that stretched north over Spain and east to Libya was ruled from Marrakech.

◆◆
PALAIS EL BAHIA
medina – east
A garden drive leads down from a busy street to this sprawling 19th-century viziers' palace. It was built by Si Moussa and his son Ba Ahmed, who served as chief ministers to three generations of Alouite sultans. A custodian will take you through a bewildering series of passages which connect a series of glittering reception rooms to the three principal courtyards: an intimate Moorish garden, a larger garden used by the viziers' wives and a vast, paved courtyard for the concubines. *Open*: officially daily 08.30–12.00 and 14.30–18.00 hrs, but in practice the palace often seems to be closed.

◆◆
PARC MÉNARA
about a mile (2km) due west of Bab Jdid

The Koutoubia's inspiring minaret

This substantial reservoir was built by the Almohads in the 12th century, to supply the walled gardens and orchards to the west of the city. In the mid-19th century an elegant pavilion was placed in the centre of the south bank, its silhouette framed against a backdrop of the Atlas mountains. On the first-floor terrace, cooled by light winds, guests at royal picnics were refreshed by the view over the tranquil sheet of water and by musical entertainments. It is still

a good spot for picnics.
Open: daily until sunset.

RAMPARTS
(a tour by horse carriage)
A line of horse-drawn carriages
can be found at the western end
of place Jemaa el Fna. They are
a treat in themselves and a
delightful way to travel out to
look at the Ménara or Majorelle
gardens. A more ambitious
itinerary would involve a
complete trot around the red
ramparts of Marrakech.
The 30-foot (9m) high walls
were built by the Almoravide
Sultan Ali ben Youssef in the
12th century, as defence against
the growing Almohad threat.
They include 200 towers and 20
gates and stretched for 10 miles
(16km). Eight centuries on, the
ramparts of sun-baked clay, still
largely follow the original
course.
Ask the driver to point out the
massive **Bab Doukkala**, the
principal western gate which,
though much restored, is the
lone survivor from the original
12th-century Almoravide walls.
On the east side you might ask
to stop at **Bab Eddebbagh** and
employ a young guide to take
you on a tour of the Marrakech
tanneries.
The southern face of the city is
occupied by the **Royal Palace**
(Palais Royal), on the site of the
12th-century Almohad kasbah.
All that can be seen are the
glittering gates as you trot
through three formal squares.
The Méchouar des Alouites is
the largest of these with the
elegant Pavillon Essaouira set
against the far wall. When the

king is not in residence you are
welcome to drive down through
the Aguedal gardens to an
Almohad pool overlooked by
two ruined pavilions.

SOUK ✓

North of crowd-filled place
Jemaa el Fna lie the various
entrances to the labryinthine
souk of Marrakech, where
everything – from impotence
charms to ghetto-blasters – is
sold. This magnificent spider's
web of commerce has a bad
reputation with tourists, but if
you hire a local guide and
agree the price beforehand, he
will protect you from the
crowds of other hustlers.
A cluster of stalls and pottery-
filled courtyards hide the arch
that marks the entrance to **rue
Souk Smarine**, the principal
shop-lined alley. From here you
can explore the **spice market** at
the entrance to the Rahba
Kédima courtyard, the old **grain
market**, and the nearby **Souk
Larzal** and **Souk Btana**, where
wool and raw skins are traded.
The old slave market (until
1912) is now known as the
Criée Berbère, a shaded
square lined with carpet and
killim stalls, where carpet
auctions are staged. There is a
concentration of jewellers off
Souk el Kebir as well as wood-
turners, leather-binders and a
distinguished horse-harness
shop. **Souk el Attarin**, the old
perfume-sellers' market leads
into a tight grid of alleys, the
Kissaria, at the heart of the
souk. Here you will find all
manner of clothes and the **Souk**

Light at the end of the souk

des Babouches, with its staggering tiered display of yellow and gilt embroidered slippers.

Souk des Teinturiers, the dyers' souk, is bright with cascading skeins of wool draped over bamboo rods to dry. In **Souks Cherratine** and **Haddadine** metalwork and carpentry shops tout their wares, and there are a number of small but well-stocked bazaars along rue Mouassine.

The Mamounia Hotel is world class

◆◆
TOMBEAUX SAADIENS
(Saadian Tombs)

medina – south

A thin passageway leads to the small enclosed cemetery on the southern side of the 12th-century Kasbah mosque. Here among rosemary hedges, slender cypress and cascading creepers are the glittering royal tombs of the Saadian sultans. Peep into the first hall with its high horseshoe arches and its floor covered by the tiled tombs of princes. Next door is the **Hall of Twelve Columns**, the overpoweringly rich mausoleum of Ahmed el Mansour (the builder of El Badia palace), its giddy dome appearing like frozen drapes of gilded lace. He lies in the

central tomb surrounded by 35 descendants. On the other side, two ornate Moorish loggias overlook a simpler hall with an interior chapel, where Ahmed el Mansour's father, mother and brother lie.

Open: daily 09.00–12.00 and 14.00–18.00 hrs. Closed Friday mornings.

Accommodation
Marrakech is well supplied with a wide range of places to stay. Centrally situated, cheaper hotels tend to get booked up early in the day.

Expensive
The **Mamounia Hotel** on avenue Bab Jdid (tel: (04) 448981) was Winston Churchill's favourite and has grown into one of the world's most celebrated and opulent hotels. Its magnificent garden and restaurants still draw all who can possibly afford to stay here. De luxe five-stars.
If you want less ostentatious comfort use the **Hotel Es Saadi** beside the casino on avenue El Qadissa (tel: (04) 448811). Five stars.

Moderate
Going slightly downmarket, choose between the efficient **Hotel Chems** on avenue Houmman el Fetouaki (tel: (04) 444813) and **Hotel Les Almoravides** on arset Djenan Lakhdar (tel: (04) 445142). Both are four star and have swimming-pools, air conditioning and charming service.

Cheap
The most characterful hotels tend to be at the centre of the

town. The two-star **Grand Hotel Tazi** on rue Bab Agnaou (tel: (04) 442452) and **Hotel de Foulcauld** on avenue El Mouahidine (tel: (04) 445499) both have amusing licensed restaurants, while the new **Hotel Islane**, right opposite the Koutoubia at 279 avenue Mohammed V (tel: (04) 440081), boasts a pizzeria on its panoramic terrace.

Restaurants

Marrakech is full of old Moorish palaces, where you can spend a lively night out watching fire-eaters, musicians and gyrating belly-dancers over your tajine and couscous. The darkest and most dramatic of these is in narrow rue Riad Zitoun el Kedim which leads south from place Jemaa el Fna. Entering the massive portals of **Restaurant Dar es Salam** (tel: (04) 423272), you emerge into a series of tiled and plastered rooms and courtyards. Otherwise try **Dar el Baroud** at 275 avenue Mohammed V (tel: (04) 445077).

Two other palace restaurants are conveniently close enough to the museum and palaces to make good lunch stops, though there will be no floor show during the day. The **Riad el Bahia** (tel: (04) 441350) and **El Gharnata** (tel: (04) 425214) restaurants are both on rue Riad Zitoun el Jdid.

There are also a handful of restaurants in Marrakech that take their cooking extremely seriously. They are very expensive, but serve delightful and intellligent variations on the usual Moroccan fare.

Restaurant Le Marrakechi (tel: (04) 423377) overlooks place Jemaa el Fna, though its entrance is at 52 rue Banques. Both **Le Marocain** and **L'Imperiale** restaurants in the Mamounia Hotel also serve exquisite food.

The other, obvious eating place for night-time Marrakech is **place Jemaa el Fna**, where you can eat potato cakes at one stall, couscous at another and brochettes at yet another. Here you are eating with the people of the town itself, in an atmosphere that feels like an endless, adult fun-fair.

Nightlife

The **Casino** (tel: (04) 488112) is the night-time heart of the new town's hotel quarter, and stages floor shows as well as gambling. The **Mamounia Hotel** also has its own gaming tables and nightclub, but the liveliest and most popular of the nightclubs is in the **Hotel N'Fis**, avenue de France (tel: (04) 448772). One night during your stay, reserve a place on one of the hotel-organised 'fantasias'. This Berber spectacle provides an evening you will never forget (see page 108).

Festivals

The **National Folklore Festival** held in Marrakech in the summer is Morocco's major fête. Make an effort to get into one of the evening events staged in El Badia palace, its gaunt and secretive walls accentuated by floodlights. In July there is a **Festival of Fantasia** to the west of the Royal Palace.

WHAT TO SEE AROUND MARRAKECH

BENI-MELLAL
120 miles (194km) northeast of Marrakech

This prosperous hillside town overlooks an irrigated plain filled with orange groves. Halfway between Fès and Marrakech, it makes a convenient stop and contains a local souk round place de la Liberté, ornamental gardens beside the Asserdoun spring, and a good view from the hilltop Ras el Ain kasbah. An exciting expedition from here would be to visit the isolated **Cascade d'Ouzoud**, a thundering three-tiered 300-foot (110m) waterfall, beneath which a series of natural pools is perfect for swimming. Despite its mesmeric appeal, it rarely draws more than a handful of Barbary apes and a few dozen backpackers. The Falls are four miles (7km) from Ait Attab village.

Accommodation

The **Hotel Chems** (tel: (03) 483460) and the **Hotel Ouzoud** (tel: (03) 483752), both four star, are efficiently managed hotels on the edge of town, beside the Marrakech road. Here you can swim and sunbathe against a backdrop of mountains.

Restaurant

The best place to eat in Beni-Mellal is at **Restaurant Hotel Al Bassatine** (tel: (03) 482247), a palatial, licensed place with liveried staff, set in the orange groves off the Marrakech road.

EL-JADIDA
125 miles (200km) northwest of Marrakech

This coastal town owes much of its old world charm to the Portuguese, who held a fortress here for 250 years. When their last garrison abandoned the town during the Moroccan siege of 1769, they left behind an intact citadel which still stands today. The town's other great attraction is a long sandy beach which stretches all the way north to Azemmour. The most famous site in the citadel is the **Portuguese cistern**, a 16th-century, vaulted, subterranean interior, lit only by a skylight and yet perfectly reflected in the few inches of water on the floor. Originally it was built as a secure munitions store, but has served in its time as a fencing school, a water cistern and a location in Orson Welles's film of *Othello*.
Open: Monday to Friday 08.00–12.30 and 14.00–18.00 hrs.

At the end of the main street in the citadel is the **Porta do Mar**, a sea gate blocked by an iron grille.

Employ a guide to take you round the battlements. There are some fine bronze cannon in the **Bastion de l'Ange**, while the **Bastion St Sebastian** is crowned by a disused synagogue. For after the Portuguese left, the city remained deserted until a Jewish trading community was settled here by the sultan in 1815. On either side of El-Jadida, literally the 'new town' there were older Muslim communities. The walled town of **Azemmour** to the north is still busy, but to the south, the 12th-century community at **Tit** is long gone, its ruins just partially restored.

Accommodation

The **Hotel Doukkala Salam**, on avenue de la Ligue Arabe (tel: (03) 343737), is the only modern, well-equipped hotel in town, and it is also now the only hotel situated on the beach front. Four stars.

Le Palais Andalous on rue Curie (tel: (03) 343745) is in the landward side of town, tucked somewhat reclusively off avenue Pasteur. It is a charming

Portuguese cistern, El-Jadida

hotel made from a Moorish courtyard palace, with distinctive bedrooms, a restaurant and a bar. Three stars.

The **Hotel de Provence** at 42 avenue Fquih Er-Rafy (tel: (03) 342347) is the pick of the cheap pensions. Two stars.

Restaurants

The seafood **Restaurant Du Port** is tucked away behind the harbourfront docks, but has a superb view overlooking the Portuguese sea walls.

Restaurant Le Tit, 2 avenue Jamia Al Arabia, the coast road north, is a slightly cheaper alternative, with which the new **El Khaima Restaurant** on avenue des Nations Unies is in competition.

ESSAOUIRA

110 miles (176km) due west of Marrakech

This 18th century walled town has a fishing harbour, sandy bay and celebrated souk of woodcarvers. It has a good choice of hotels and restaurants though the fairly consistent sea breeze is more useful to windsurfers than sunbathers. Essaouira is an ancient site of trade, probably known to Phoenician merchants as early as the 7th century BC. Indeed the Mogadors, the name for the small group of offshore islands, is almost certainly derived from the word 'migdol', which is Phoenician for a look-out tower.

The present town was entirely rebuilt in the 18th century by Sultan Sidi Mohammed, who wanted to concentrate all external shipping trade in one town so that it could be controlled easily. He employed his French court architect who gave Essaouira a distinctive look by freely drawing upon both classical and Moorish traditions. This is especially evident in the handsome harbour gate in the centre of the fortified port. The attraction of the bustling fishing port is greatly enchanced by the quayside boat-builders and the al fresco fish grilling and makeshift restaurants.

From the central, café-lined place Moulay Hassan it is just a short stroll to reach the **Skala de la Ville**. This elegant coastal artillery battery, with its round north bastion and long line of bronze cannon, looks west out over the rocky shore. The pebble-floored lower courtyard and its barrel-vaulted storerooms have been turned into a souk of woodcarvers. Both here and throughout the town you will find workshops that carve the knotty root boles of the thuja tree to make a delightful assortment of boxes, backgammon sets, bowls and trays. Ebony, mother-of-pearl and lemonwood are also employed to make complex geometrical marquetry, a traditional form of furniture decoration.

The ex-French town hall on rue Derb Laalouj (once a pasha's residence) has been turned into a small **Folklore Museum** (**Museum Sidi Mohammed Ibn Abdellah**), housing an interesting collection of musical instruments.

Currently closed for restoration (usual hours: 09.00–12.00 and 14.30–18.00 hrs).

Rue Derb Laalouj leads down to the colonnaded avenue de l'Istiqlal, the elegant central thoroughfare of the town, behind which lurk a number of courtyard markets. The more sophisticated shops and bazaars are grouped near place Moulay Hassan and by the museum.

Accommodation

The **Hotel des Iles**, boulevard Mohammed V (tel: (04) 472329), tucked between the beach and the southern bastion of the medina, is Essaouira's smartest hotel and the only one with a pool. Four stars.

High and dry in Essaouira harbour

The **Hotel Tafoukt** (tel: (04) 472504) is also on boulevard Mohammed V, the coast road, but is a simpler and cheaper establishment overlooking a better part of the beach. Three stars.

Inside the medina there are any number of cheaper hotels to choose from. The two-star **Hotel Sahara** (tel: (04) 472292) is the cleanest and most hygienic of these.

Restaurants
In addition to good restaurants in the des Iles and Tafoukt hotels, there are two lively, licensed seafood restaurants to visit here. The terrace of the **Chalet de la Plage**, at the town end of the beach, is washed by the tide and a good place for catching the sunset. The **Port de Pêche**, at the far end of the harbour, can almost be mistaken for a fishing boat, but serves a multitude of different dishes and an excellent *menu du jour*.

◆
KASBAH-DE-BOULÂOUANE
about 100 miles (160km) north of Marrakech
This superb fortress crowns a hill overlooking the meandering course of the River Oum er Rbia. It was built by Sultan Moulay Ismaïl in the early 18th century and now stands empty and little visited. You can walk around its curtain walls, explore underground storage chambers and a back tunnel, and identify the ruined palace and baths. Set in the centre of a wine-growing region, it lies in the hamlet of Boulâouane, half an hour off the dull road between Casablanca and Marrakech.

◆ OUALIDIA

about 125 miles (200km) northwest of Marrakech

The sandy lagoon below the small beach resort of Oualidia provides safe swimming out of reach of the currents of the Atlantic Ocean. The village is quiet and largely undiscovered by foreign tourists.

There are a couple of beach-front motels and campsites, which rent out watersports equipment, while the two hotels on the hill, the one-star **Auberge de La Lagune** (tel: (03) 346477 and the smarter, two-star **Hotel Hippocampe** (tel: (03) 346499) are renowned for their cooking. Equidistant from Safi, El-Jadida and Kasbah Boulâouane, Oualidia is also well placed for cultural forays.

◆ OUKAÏMEDEN

A third of the way along the Ourika valley (see page 79) there is a turning up a mountain road that in 18 miles (30km) twists up to the dizzy heights of Mount Oukaïmeden. The rocky bowl beneath the peak shelters a small resort that offers skiing in winter and hiking throughout the rest of the year. The peak snow conditions are usually in February and March, though the view alone is worth the drive. There are two Alpine chalet-style hotels, the **Hotel Juju** (tel: (04) 459005) and **Hotel Imlil** (tel: (04) 459132), with rental ski facilities and restaurants in the hotels.

◆ SAFI

97 miles (157km) northwest of Marrakech

This busy Atlantic fishing port has a delightful old town, but the lack of beaches and the proximity of the chemical works puts it off the main tourist map. The Portuguese occupied the town in the 16th century and left behind a **gothic chapel**, a coastal fort, now known as the **Dar el Bahr** and the round bastions of the hilltop **Kechla fortress** (where a museum of ceramics is housed).

All three open: 09.00–12.00 and 15.00–18.00 hrs.

In addition you can wander round the ramparts, admire the 18th-century docks and the modern 200-strong fishing fleet, and walk up the principal street of the old town, rue du Souk, to reach Bab Chaabah and the famous **potteries** of Safi, producing colourful glazed ceramics, mostly salt glaze blue on a white ground with abstract designs.

Accommodation

Stay at either the **Safir** on avenue Zenktouni (tel: (04) 464299), or the more modest **De L'Atlantide** at 50 rue Chaouki (tel: (04) 462160). Both 4 stars.

◆◆ TELOUET and TIZI-N-TICHKA

High Atlas, about 125 miles (200km) from Marrakech

The road from Marrakech to Ouarzazate crosses the High Atlas peaks at the **Tizi-n-Tichka pass**. It is less alarming than the Tizi-n-Test route to Taroudannt

Competing with the peaks of the High Atlas, pottery stalls are a ubiquitous attraction

(see next entry), but the added width of the road is often taken up by over-ambitious mineral drinks salesmen.

There is no shortage of dramatic views, hairpin bends and alarming potential drops either.

Just 2½ miles (4km) south of the Tizi-n-Tichka summit keep a look-out for the turning to **Telouet**. The 13-mile (21km) dead-end drive leads directly to the decaying mass of a **kasbah**, once the citadel of the Glaoui. This clan of highland Berbers had risen to power as officials of the sultan at the turn of the century. They then enormously expanded their influence by forging an early alliance with the French colonial regime and were made unofficial viceroys of southern Morocco.

The resident custodians take tours through the principal reception rooms of the kasbah, which – though decayed – still reek of decadent splendour. From the roof there are serene views over the unspoiled mountain valley.

A glittering prize from the mountains

♦♦♦
TIZI-N-TEST and TIN-MAL ✓

High Atlas
This route twists across the High Atlas mountains on an exhilarating and at times frankly alarming 125-mile (200km) drive between the two walled cities of Marrakech and Taroudannt. The village of **Imlil**, 10 miles (17km) up a track from Asni and the main road, is a centre for mountain climbing in the surrounding **Toubkal National Park** which includes the highest peak in North

Africa, Jbel Toubkal, at 13,672 feet (4,167m).

After you pass the roadside village of Ijoukak, look out for the hilltop fortress of **Agadir n'Gouf**, built by a powerful tribal lord at the turn of the century to guard his prized stable of Arab horses. Two miles (3km) further south, a turning across the river leads to the magnificent half-ruined **Great Mosque of Tin-Mal**. This historic 12th-century Almohad shrine is the only mosque a non-Muslim may enter in Morocco, though you will find it closed on Fridays for the village prayers. It marks the site where the founder of the Almohad dynasty, Ibn Tumert, first established the puritanical reform movement that swept across North Africa and Spain. The hamlet of **Idni** marks the beginning of the really hair-raising part of the drive, a possible turning-point if you are just out for the day.

Accommodation
You can eat, swim, chat to monkeys and stay in one of 20 bedrooms at the **Grand Hotel du Toubkal** in Asni (tel: 3 Par Marrakech – no direct dialling). Three stars.
Further up the pass, the hamlet of Ouirgane has two well-known and popular hotels. On one side of the mountain stream is the truly luxurious four-star **Résidence La Roseraie** (tel: (04) 432094) with a stable of Arab horses. On the other, sits the distinctive two-star **Au Sanglier Qui Fume**, 'the smoking boar' (tel: 9 – no direct dialling).

◆◆
VALLÉE DE L'OURIKA
about 20 miles (33km) south of Marrakech

This narrow mountain valley makes a delightful break from the heat and activity of Marrakech. The steep, red hills, half-covered in stunted pines, rise barren above the vivid green valley floor, with its irrigated riverside gardens. Cool mountain breezes rustle the fruit trees grown in neat, terraced orchards and the silver leaves of aspen and the bright oleander flowers along the Ourika river bed.

The Monday market at **Tnine-de-l'Ourika** is the major event of the week, but there is a profusion of roadside stalls selling pottery and fossils throughout the week. Ask your guide or taxi-driver to show you the water-powered mill on the road up to **Setti Fatma** at the head of the valley. The road has been washed away just before you reach the hamlet, and having walked the last half mile (1km) you can reward yourself with river-cooled soft drinks before walking uphill to a series of slight waterfalls.

Restaurants

The four-star **Ourika Hotel** (tel: (04) 433993) makes a comfortable overnight base, but it is more stimulating to eat in one of the valley's other restaurants. The elaborate dining room of the **Lion de l'Ourika**, the cheaper **Auberge Marquis** or the **Kasbah Restaurant** in a converted palace are all within a few miles of one another.

AGADIR, OUARZAZATE AND THE SOUTH

The southern half of Morocco is largely covered by a barren, rocky plain, the beginning of the Sahara desert. A handful of oasis river valleys thread verdant lifelines deep into the inhospitable terrain, and the Anti-Atlas mountains shelter a population of farmers and shepherds.

The landscape is vast and majestic in its severity and is disturbed only by the contrasting intimacy of the oasis valleys colonised by millions of palm trees. Beneath these natural sunshades the industrious population grows fruit, nuts and vegetables in carefully watered gardens, sticking fiercely to a tradition of survival worked out over thousands of years. The towns and villages, often dominated by tapering forts known as kasbahs, are made from the earth itself and blend in seamlessly with their surroundings. Deep in the oasis valleys, entire villages still hide within defensive walls, echoing a historical need to protect themselves from tribes of aggressive nomads. To enter one of these ksour, as they are called, is to walk into a maze of narrow alleys and successive pools of deep cool shade and invigorating bright sunshine. **Agadir** is Morocco's largest and most popular beach resort. It is also the calmest and least demanding city, from where you can explore the western fringes of the Sahara. **Ouarzazate** has emerged as the inland counterfoil to Agadir and the eastern base for the desert south. Both Agadir and Ouarzazate have airports, car rental facilities, tour agents and a full range of glittering hotels to cater for those seeking almost guaranteed winter sun.

The old walled cities of **Taroudannt** and **Tiznit** with their famous covered souks are about two hours from Agadir. Other possible daytrips include the drive up to **Imouzzer-Ida-Outanan**, the **Sidi-Rbat** nature reserve, the Saturday market at **Goulimine** (**Guelmine**), the oasis of **Tiout** and the agadir of **Amtoudi**. It would be a pity not to stay at **Tafraout** and have a whole day free to walk in the surrounding oases and rock valleys.

Going east to Ouarzazate you have a number of dramatic alternatives. Just west there is **Aït-Benhaddou**, the most famous kasbah village in southern Morocco. Due south the kasbah- and palm-strewn **Dra valley** leads to the hotels in **Zagora** from where you can take camel treks. East from Ouarzazate are the twin attractions of the **Dadès** and **Todra gorges**, before passing the spring-fed **Blue Meski pool** (**Source Bleue de Meski**) on your way to **Erfoud**. This small town at the centre of the Tafilalt oasis is the destination for those determined to catch a desert dawn at the golden dunes of **Erg Chebbi**.

Sunset at Agadir beach, the end of another hard day's relaxation

AGADIR

Year-round sunshine, a wide, sandy bay set against a backdrop of hills, and a compact, elegant hotel quarter have made Agadir the country's principal resort. The **town beach** is one of the safest swimming beaches on the Atlantic coast, which elsewhere contains some fearsome currents and undertow. It is firmly established as Agadir's principal attraction – at once a sporting playground, a social promenade and a place for mesmeric relaxation.

European visitors of a different kind – merchants – were already visiting Agadir in the 15th century. In the first part of the 16th century, it was an important Portuguese trading post until the Portuguese fort there fell to the Saadians in 1542. There followed 120 years of prosperity under the Saadian rulers, which declined with the coming of the Alouite sultans and ended with the destruction of the port by Sidi Mohammed in 1760. Not until the French Protectorate did the town recover some of its prosperity.

There is little in the way of sights in Agadir, as the old town was completely destroyed in an earthquake in 1960. The city centre is a classic piece of modern town planning, with wide boulevards, public gardens and central shopping malls. The **kasbah** which crowns the hill to the north was also shattered and has been left as a memorial to the disaster. Its 18th-century gatehouse has

a bilingual inscription, in Dutch (a momento of 18th-century Dutch trading activity) and Arabic, but the chief reason for the climb is the panoramic view. Below the kasbah, the **port** shelters a considerable sardine-fishing fleet. Their catch can be sampled at the grill-cafés whose tables cluster round the dock gates. On the opposite side of the city a colourful and animated **market** takes place in a modern kasbah on rue Chari el Hamra. Of interest is the **Valley of the Birds** which includes a zoo, aviary, waterfall and playground and is ideal for children. There is also a new **folk art museum** next to the outdoor theatre.

Accommodation
In the hotel quarter, between boulevard Mohammed V, boulevard du 20 Août and the beach, you will find the principal resort hotels, some two dozen of them.

Expensive
Those with the best position and sporting facilities are the **Club Med** (tel: (08) 840542) and the **PLM Les Dunes d'Or** (tel: (08) 840150), both right on the beach.

The four-star **Hotel Les Almohades** (tel: (08) 840233) near by is a beautiful establishment with attentive service. The four-star **Hotel Sahara** (tel: (08) 840660) also has a good sea view.

Well placed between beach and town is the **Hotel Salam** (tel: (08) 840840). Friendly and luxurious. Three stars.

A golden moment at an Agadir café

Moderate

All of the expensive resort hotels are huge, and it is only by dropping down the price scale that hotels begin to become more intimate. This does mean moving further from the beach, though it must be said that it is still only a five-minute walk away.

The three-star **Hotel Aladin** on rue de la Jeunesse (tel: (08) 843228) has 60 rooms and charming staff. Three stars. **Hotel les Palmiers** on boulevard du Prince Héritier Sidi Mohammed (tel: (08) 843719) is smaller still but has a popular nightclub. Two stars.

Cheap

For a tighter budget, the cheapest hotels are to be found along rue Allal ben Abdellah as you walk up to the bus station. Particularly clean and efficient is the one-star, 16-room **Hotel El Bahia** (tel: (08) 822724).

Restaurants

La Langouste (tel: (08) 823636) and **Marine Heim** are two of the more popular restaurants in the hotel quarter, but in general the food in Agadir suffers from blandness. For a more individual night out with a Moroccan flavour try **Les Arcades** at 1 avenue Allal ben Abdellah (tel: (08) 823706) or the **Yacht Club** restaurant (tel: (08) 823095), within the port gates, where the emphasis is heavily on fish. There are cheap grill-cafés near the main bus station, avenue Yaacoub Mansour.

Nightlife

The **Rendezvous** is the most popular independent nightclub in town, though most tourist social life revolves around the floor shows, cabarets and discothèques of the major hotels listed above. The hotels

Atlas and Sahara usually have live bands playing until around 23.00 hrs, but the **Byblos** nightclub in the PLM Les Dunes d'Or is widely considered the most lively.

Shopping

Before bargaining in the Agadir bazaars or setting off for the souks in Taroudannt or Tiznit, have a look at the prices in the state craft showrooms on boulevard du 29 Février and rue Mehdi Ibn Tumert. Agadir has no tradition of specialisation in any particular craft, but there is a good range of woodwork from nearby Essaouira, and local fossils. Picnic supplies, wine and spirits can be bought from the Uniprix supermarket on place Hassan II.

Special Events

Ask your hotel or a travel agent in the town to book you in for a fantasia, an evening of exciting folklore entertainment beneath the stars.

WHAT TO SEE FROM AGADIR

◆◆
AMTOUDI

Anti-Atlas, about 60 miles (100km) inland from Goulimine
The agadir (the Berber word for a communal fortified granary) at Amtoudi is one of the oldest and most dramatic of all the fortified granaries in the Anti-Atlas mountains. Its natural defensive position has been strengthened by a stout gateway, which used to guard the grain and stores of the

nomadic Iznaguen tribe. Approached off the back road to the Tata oasis, the mountain track passes up a gorge studded with palms and rock pools before reaching an enterprising café. Here donkeys can be rented for the ascent and a meal ordered to be ready on your return.

◆
GOULIMINE (GUELMIME)

about 115 miles (185km) south of Agadir
This large, dusty town on the edge of the Western Sahara was once renowned for its market, frequented by the nomadic blue tribes of the Western Sahara. Though the days of camel transport and the trans-Saharan caravan trade are long gone, the Saturday market remains a popular event for locals and coachloads of tourists. Day trips from Agadir often include lunch in the nearby oasis palmery of Aït-Boukha, where guedra, an erotic dance performed on their knees by the women of the Sahara, is also demonstrated.

Accommodation

Goulimine's best hotel is the two-star **Hotel Salam** (tel: (08) 872057), which also stages guedra dancing on Saturday evenings.

Festivals

The nearby Asrir oasis celebrates the moussem of Sidi Mohammed Ben Amar in early June, while the moussem of Sidi Laghazi at Goulimine is held later in the month.

◆◆
IMOUZZER-IDA-OUTANAN
about 30 miles (50km) north of Agadir

This pretty highland village lies at the head of so-called 'banana valley', which twists up beside a palm-lined mountain stream (past the delightfully sited **Tafrite Restaurant**). The three-star **Hotel des Cascades** (tel: 16 – no direct dialling) here is elegant and serene, a far cry from the bustle of Agadir and would make a good base for a few days' walking. The nearby waterfalls are the major attraction however, impressive more for the beauty of the rock formation and pools than for the trickle of descending water.

Market day, Imouzzer-Ida-Outanan

◆
LA'YOUNE
about 295 miles (475km) south of Goulimine

This, the administrative capital of the Western Sahara, lies astride a brackish lagoon fringed with sand dunes. It has grown in 40 years from a lone outpost of the Spanish Foreign Legion to a city of 100,000 with its own airport and monumental town centre. From the city, landrover excursions leave for the nearby beach, the spring at the oasis of Lemsid, the old British trading post at Tarfaya, the Spanish fortress of Dchira, and the ruined palace of the Blue Sultan Ma el Ainin – leader of resistance against the French at Smara.

Accommodation

The **Parador**, rue Okbaa Ibn Nafeh (tel: (08) 894500) and **Hotel Al Massira Khadra**, rue de la Mecque (tel: (08) 894225) are both elegant and luxurious hotels, complete with much-needed swimming-pools. Both five stars.

◆

SIDI-IFNI
102 miles (165km) south of Agadir

In 1969 the Spanish finally quit the small colonial enclave of Sidi-Ifni. They left behind a ring of military barracks, an airbase, a port accessible only by cable-car, and a coastal town filled with art deco architecture, now slowly decaying in the prevailing sea mist. The hotels **Belle Vue** and **Beau Rivage** provide meals, drinks and basic accommodation.

◆◆

SIDI-RBAT
about 25 miles (40km) south of Agadir

Local legend has it that Jonah was disgorged by the whale on to this very beach, named after the Muslim saint whose tomb rises at one end. Behind the beach, a nature reserve occupies a bird-covered lagoon and an area of dunes, rock cliffs and rough grazing. There have long been schemes afoot to reintroduce extinct species here, but little seems to change. The basic facilities include a campsite, a restaurant and spartan rooms.

◆◆◆

TAFRAOUT
Anti-Atlas, 94 miles (144km) east of Tiznit

Tafraout is the market town for the farmers of the Ammeln oasis valley, high up in the Anti-Atlas mountains east of Agadir. Its surprising air of prosperity is due to the industrious nature of the population, many of whom leave the village to become shopkeepers throughout Morocco and return wealthy.

The attraction for visitors lies in walking among the patches of green garden, shaded by almond and palm groves and set in a near lunar landscape of eroded, volcanic rocks beneath the vertical escarpment of Jbel Lekst. The journey from Agadir is exhilarating as well. Leaving behind the market gardens of the Sous valley, the route winds through arid grazing land dotted with thuja, the hardy and indigenous thorn tree of the region. Above the thuja line, it climbs through striking mountain scenery studded with characteristic stone farmhouses and dramatic ruined hilltop agadirs.

Accommodation and Restaurant

The **Hotel les Amandiers** (tel: (08) 800008), whose kasbah silhouette overlooks the town, is cool and comfortable, with an excellent dining-room. Four stars.

There are also two cheap, basic hotels in the centre, the **Tangier** and **Redouane**, and an amusing tented, garden restaurant, **L'Etoile du Sud**.

Festivals

A festival in mid to late February celebrates the delicate pink and white blossoming of the almond trees.

TALIOUINE and TAZENAKHT

about 125 and 175 miles (200 and 280km) respectively, east of Agadir

Between Agadir and Ouarzazate, there are good reasons to stop at both these roadside towns. **Taliouine** is at the centre of a delightful mountain valley, which has a scattering of earth-built villages among its palmery and stone hamlets perched on the hilltops. The ruined **Glaoui kasbah**, built by the local ruling family around the turn of the century, is the central attraction and can be viewed from the terrace of the elegant neighbouring **Hotel Ibn Tumert** (tel: 30 – no direct dialling). The hotel has a pool, bar and restaurant. The **Caravan Salam** restaurant (tel: 55) is a popular lunch-stop. Continuing east, **Tazenakht**, surrounded by an arid highland plateau, is celebrated as the market for bright, boldly patterned Ouzguita carpets. These are made by the local Ouzguita tribe and are proudly displayed by the roadside, in the artisan co-operative square and in more exclusive boutiques.

TARHAZOUT

10 miles (16km) north of Agadir

At Tarhazout beach, the sea is usually vigorous and the sands less crowded than those of Agadir itself. It is the haunt of surfers, who chase the waves here and in the smaller bays further north. Tarhazout has no hotels, just a campsite and a terraced restaurant, the **Sables d'Or**.

TAROUDANNT

50 miles (80km) east of Agadir

This walled city, surrounded by groves of olive and orange, is the ancient capital of the Sous valley (Plaine du Sous) and briefly served as the national capital under the Saadian dynasty in the 16th century. A horse-drawn carriage tour of the ochre, battlemented walls, stopping at the tannery by Bab Khemis gate, naturally ends at the centre of town, the café-lined place Assareg. From here you can nip into the bar of the Hotel Taroudannt for a beer or explore the souk, which sells a multitude of traditional crafts as well as local specialities such as fox-skins, stone carvings and leather sandals.

Accommodation

Just outside Taroudannt is the **Gazelle d'Or** hotel (tel: (08) 852039), one of the most exclusive hotels in the world. Its lawns are hand-clipped, and the hotel boasts riding stables and a gastronomic restaurant but is reluctant to accept telephone bookings or welcome outsiders. Five stars. The **Hotel Palais Salaam** (tel: (08) 852312) is tucked just inside the city walls, combining the dignified remnants of an old palace with modern conveniences such as

Taroudannt's walls rise from the groves

swimming-pools and a friendly management. Four stars.

The **Hotel Saadiens**, on rue Bordj Ennasim (tel: (08) 852589), is a smaller and cheaper alternative. Two stars.

◆
TIOUT
Sous valley, about 15 miles (25km) from Taroudannt
Nestling against the Anti-Atlas foothills on the southern edge of the Sous valley (Plaine du Sous), this oasis palmery is composed of five hamlets, overlooked by a ruinous Glaoui kasbah. Hidden among the palm trees are saints' tombs, springs and the usual, carefully tended network of irrigation channels.

◆◆
TIZNIT
57 miles (93km) south of Agadir
At the turn of the century this pink-walled city on the edge of the Sahara was famous for its jewellers and dancing girls and as the capital of El Hiba, the Blue Sultan, who led a spirited rebellion against the French in 1912-13.

The full three-mile (5km) circuit of walls is in fine condition and the Gate of Three Windows is the principal entrance into the **mechouar**, a café-lined main square bordered by the alleyways of the jewellers' market. In the smaller place du Pasha, El Hiba was acclaimed sultan by the blue-robed tribes of the desert. Passing the minaret of the **Great Mosque**, you reach a pool, sacred to the memory of Lalla Tiznit, a local saint who was a reformed prostitute.

The modest town beach of **Sidi-Moussa-Aglou**, 10½ miles (17km) away, has a cheap motel and a local restaurant where the fish tajine is excellent. By night, in the Tiznit Hotel in town, there is a display of traditional dancing (18.00–20.00 hrs).

Accommodation

The **Tiznit Hotel** (tel: (08) 862411) stands beside the main road on the roundabout just outside town. It has a nightclub, a Moorish dining-room and rooms overlooking the courtyard garden and swimming-pool. Three stars. For those on a tight budget there are a number of basic hotels around the mechouar.

Festivals

In August the moussem of Sidi Abderrahman takes place in Tiznit, followed by a six-day acrobat's fête at the zaouia of Sidi Ahmed ou Moussa beginning on the third Thursday of the month.

OUARZAZATE

This once lonely but strategic fortress is now a fully-fledged resort, its central position making it ideal for exploring the sites of southeastern Morocco. Not only does it now boast dozens of luxury hotels, a nearby hydro scheme to provide water and electricity for them, an airport, a golf course, and a zoo, but increasing numbers of film-makers, attracted by the climate and landscape, are fast creating a new industry as well.

The principal site of the town, surrounded by cafés and carpet showrooms, is the showy, 19th-century **kasbah of Taourirt**. From here the local

Ouarzazate is not a desert mirage

governing family, the Glaoui,
lorded it over the oasis valleys.
The courtyard holds a Krupp-
manufactured German cannon,
presented to them by Sultan
Moulay Hassan, and above the
craft workshops are two
original, ornately decorated
chambers.
Open: daily 08.00–18.00 hrs.

Accommodation

The best hotel in Ouarzazate is
the **Hotel Riad Salam** (tel: (04)
882206) in the hotel quarter. It
is designed as an imitation
kasbah, surrounded by
gardens, and has 70 spacious
double rooms. Four stars.
The **PLM Hotel Karam Palace**
(tel: (04) 882522) is built around
a large swimming-pool and has
impressive sporting facilities.
A little more simple is the **Hotel
Tichka Salam** (tel: (04)
882206), where priority is given
to quiet but attentive service. It
is also in the hotel quarter.
Three stars.
The cheaper hotels, like the **Es
Salaam** and the **Royal**, nestle
round **Chez Dimitri Restaruant**
on boulevard Mohammed V.

WHAT TO SEE FROM OUARZAZATE

◆◆
AÏT-BENHADDOU
*18½ miles (30km) northwest of
Ouarzazate*
The fame of this village has
spread far, for it has featured in
half a dozen major films,
numerous advertisements and
thousands of posters. A
battlemented outer wall, added
by a film company, encloses a
nest of four-square kasbahs

with decorated tapering towers,
crowned by a ruined agadir
above the village.
Aït-Benhaddou was once
astride one of the principal
routes across the High Atlas
mountains, but the village has
discovered new commercial
possibilities. Donkeys wait by
the river bank to take visitors
across the Oued Mellah where
they are greeted by smiling
children, who for a
consideration will act as voluble
and charming guides. On your
way back to the car park there
are many stalls of beautiful local
fossils.

EL-KELAA-MGOUNA
*about 60 miles (95km) east of
Ouarzazate*
On the junction of the Dadès
and Mgouna river valleys is this
small arcaded town two hours'
drive from Ouarzazate, and a
convenient base for exploring
the magnificent and lavishly
decorated kasbahs of the
region. It is also celebrated for
its rosewater, the basic
component for most scents and
colognes. At this height, about
6,000 feet (2,000m) above sea-
level, roses are grown as
profitable hedgerows and are
harvested in May when a
celebratory festival is staged.
The petals are either dried to
make pot-pourri or distilled in
the local plant. The hilltop
Roses du Dadès Hotel (tel:
(04) 883807) organises short
landrover tours, a whole
day's riding or a two-day
expedition, including dinner
and a bed in the romantic
Taourirt kasbah.

Carpets to the left of them, carpets to the right; Berber rugs and killims in authentic designs arrayed to dazzle and beguile passers by

◆◆
ERFOUD
about 180 miles (290km) east of Ouarzazate

This desert town, with its regular grid of dusty red houses, was established by the French Foreign Legion as the administrative centre for the Tafilalt oasis, a group of palmeries supporting 700,000 palm trees on the banks of the Oued Ziz. The town square is bordered by the date and fossil market and is overlooked by Bordj Est (Fort East), a hilltop eyrie with magnificent views over the palm gardens. Clustered round Erfoud are dozens of mysterious Tafilalt ksar – villages with regular, blank, outer walls and dark labyrinthine interiors. **Rissani**, with its Thursday and Sunday market, has expanded into a sizeable village and borders the ruins of **Sijilmassa**, a near-legendary medieval city which flourished on the profits of the trans-Saharan caravan trade. Just south, beside the oasis ringroad, is **Ksar Akbar**, a 19th-century royal treasury. Close by is the restored **shrine** of Moulay Ali Cherif (the founder of the reigning Alouite dynasty), and a mile (2km) further on, the melancholic ruins of a governor's palace, **Ksar Oulad Abdelhalim**.

Accommodation

The roadside four-star **Hotel Salon** (tel: (05) 576424) is built in open-plan, motel style and is more efficient than the plush mid-town three-star **Hotel Tafilalt** on avenue Moulay Ismaïl (tel: (05) 576535).

ERG CHEBBI
about 30 miles (50km) southeast of Erfoud
This ridge of golden sand dunes is one of the most romantic and oft-filmed landscapes in Morocco. The dunes are best seen at dawn or dusk, when refracted sunlight picks out the subtle contours of the sand. In the clear light of a desert morning the distant peaks of the High Atlas appear on the fast-changing horizon.

Accommodation
The main Erfoud hotels run Landrover tours, which may include a night spent in the **Hotel des Palmiers** in the nearby hamlet of Merzouga or in a simple dune-side café. The high dune behind the hotel is much frequented by sand skiers.

GORGES DU DADÈS
High Atlas
The River Dadès has cut a dark, vertical gorge through the High Atlas mountains, 15 miles (25km) up the valley from Boumalne-Dadès. The twisting drive up the narrow valley is a treat in itself. The dense green of garden plots, rustled by cool winds from the gorge and fed by the stream, contrasts intensely with the varying gold and purple of the barren hills and soil around. The most celebrated view is at the **Kasbah of the Rocks**, where a battlemented hamlet is overawed by a mountainside of smooth, eroded volcanic shapes.

The long and winding road clings to the edge of the Dadès gorge

See also **Peace and Quiet** page 97.

Todra Gorge cuts a swathe

Accommodation

The town of Boumalne-Dadès at the entrance to the valley offers the luxurious hilltop terraces of the four-star **El Madayeq Hotel** (tel: (04) 834031) or the cheaper roadside **Hotel Les Voix des Oiseaux** (tel: (04) 834138). One star.

In addition, there are a number of cheap hotels in the valley, including the **Kasbah de la**

Vieille Tradition and the **Auberge des Gorges du Dadès**. These and a handful of other restaurants prepare midday and evening meals for passing visitors as well.

◆◆
GORGES DU TODRA
High Atlas

North of the palmery of Tinerhir/Tineghir, with its hilltop Glaoui kasbah and native market, 104 miles (170km) east of Ouarzazate, a road follows the River Todra upstream. The tapering valley road stops at the Hotel Mansour, beyond which you can proceed up the almost dry river bed to reach the deepest and narrowest section of the gorge, an awesome vertical gash cut through the mountains. The natural majesty of the immense, sheer, canyon walls, the clear mountain stream and the long walks available have made it a favourite location for campers and adventure tours.

Accommodation

The most comfortable hotel in this region is the four-star **Hotel Sargho** (tel: (04) 834181), beside the kasbah in Tinerhir (Tineghir). In summer its swimming-pool is most welcome, but in winter you could economise by staying at the two-star **Hotel Todgha** (tel: (04) 834249), a distinctively quirky mid-town alternative. In the river valley there are a number of camping sites, such as that at the 'Source of the Sacred Fish', and in the gorge itself there are two basic hotels with restaurants.

◆◆
SOURCE BLEUE DE MESKI

about 30 miles (50km) north of Erfoud

If you have ever wanted to swim in the desert in a pool of spring water brimming with carp, don't miss out on Meski. This spring-fed rock pool was built by the French Foreign Legion, who wanted to avoid the snakes and bilharzia

worms that they occasionally found in the water of the oasis valleys. There is a popular campsite and restaurant beside the pool, while on the other side of the River Ziz are the ruins of **Ksar Meski**, a native village destroyed in tribal warfare at the turn of the century.

Accommodation

The town of Er-Rachidia, 13½ miles (22km) north of Meski, has a number of hotels, including the luxury riverside **Hotel Rissani** (tel: (05) 572186), whose restaurant has an excellent reputation.

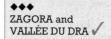

◆◆◆
ZAGORA and VALLÉE DU DRA ✓

104 miles (168km) southeast of Ouarzazate

The journey south from Ouarzazate to Zagora is one of the most spectacular drives in southern Morocco. Having crossed the western edge of the barren slopes of the Jebet Sorhino massif at the Tizi-n-Tinififft pass, the road descends into the Dra valley at **Agdz**, a village of cafés and opulent displays of bold carpets. From here the Dra valley stretches south like a miniature Nile. The empty desert hills stride immutably above the narrow green valley of palms, out of which rise an astonishing series of mud-built villages and isolated kasbahs.

The small modern town of **Zagora** appears rather drab in contrast to the splendid scenery, but its full range of hotels makes it a useful base. Though the town's bazaar is always open, the local market days are Wednesday and Sunday. In the immediate palmery you can walk to a ruined 11th-century Amoravide fortress and to the 'Kasbah of the Jews' at **Amazraou** to the south.

Further south, **Tamgrout** is famed for its everyday green pottery and medieval Islamic library. The sand dunes of **Tinfou** and the quiet village of **Mhamid** mark the southernmost extremity of the Dra where it meets the great Sahara.

Further adventures can be had **camel riding**, which you can arrange at any of the main Zagora hotels. If you are used to riding horses, watch out for the lurching, three-stage rise of a seated camel. Choose the trip to suit yourself, anything from a brief hour's ramble outside Amazraou, to a two-day ride, with dinner and a night spent under canvas beneath the numbing beauty and clarity of the star-studded Saharan sky.

Accommodation
The **Hotel PLM Reda** (tel: (04) 847249) is now the plushest hotel in Zagora, though the older **Hotel Tinsouline** (tel: (04) 847252) retains much of its charm. Both four stars.

Of the cheaper hotels on avenue Mohammed V, the **Hotel Vallée du Dra** is the best while the garden of the four-star **Hotel La Fibule du Dra** provides a memorable setting for a meal.

Waiting for a fare: the ship of the desert, the captain and his mate

PEACE AND QUIET

Countryside and Wildlife in Morocco

by Paul Sterry

Morocco is a country of extraordinary contrasts. Behind the Atlantic coast there are wetlands and marshes, while further inland agricultural plains give way to ranges of mountains, some of their higher slopes cloaked in forests of cedar or cork oak. Beyond lies the Sahara.

The range of habitats is reflected in the wealth and diversity of Moroccan wildlife. In summer the coastal wetlands are home to breeding species, and in winter they receive tens of thousands of migrants from Europe. The forests shelter woodland birds and colourful flowers, some of which will be familiar to visitors from southern Europe, while the deserts are home to more exclusive animals, typical of North Africa.

Morocco also lies on the most important route for birds migrating between Western Europe and Africa. The Straits of Gibraltar near Tanger concentrate and funnel the birds, which want to cross the water at the narrowest point. Astonishing numbers can be seen on some days in spring and autumn.

Along the Coast

Large numbers of sea birds can be seen offshore, especially during migration times in spring and autumn. Onshore winds provide the best weather conditions for sea-watching and headlands such as Cap Rhir near Agadir and Cap Blanc north of Oualidia are particularly good.

Inland and to the south of Rabat, there are cork oak woodlands with colourful flowers such as cistuses, rosemary, tree heathers and brooms, together with a wide variety of spring orchids such as naked man orchid, tongue orchid, mirror orchid and yellow bee orchid – altogether reminiscent of Mediterranean Europe. Unusual woodland birds include the double-spurred francolin – a speciality of the area. These partridge-like birds are sometimes seen in pairs feeding on the ground. Common bulbuls and black-headed bush shrikes highlight the fact that you are in Africa, although golden orioles and short-toed treecreepers are more familiar European species.

Freshwater pools – often seasonal – wetlands and saltpans are a feature of many stretches of coast. Depending on the water level and degree of disturbance, visitors can expect to find egrets and storks and sometimes flamingos.

In and Around Towns and Cities

Although city life is not compatible with many forms of wildlife, a surprisingly wide range of creatures can be found in Moroccan towns. Colourful butterflies visit flowers in parks and gardens, geckos live in the houses and several species of

PEACE AND QUIET

Nesting on the ruins in Meknès...

Geckos

Geckos are a familiar sight in houses and on walls in many parts of Morocco. These flat-looking lizards have large eyes with vertical pupils which they use to hunt insects at night. They are superb climbers: they have claws on their feet and suckers on their toes and hence they can run up walls and across ceilings. They can also change colour to suit their surroundings, making them altogether creatures to be admired rather than taken for granted. In fact, their hunting abilities are so good that they should be regarded as the ultimate in environment-friendly insect deterrents.

birds have adapted to live side by side with man – some of them benefiting from his presence. For example, little swifts can be seen hunting for insects in spring and summer over most Moroccan towns. House buntings, as their name suggests, are also easily seen, and gardens may harbour common bulbuls and migrants in spring and autumn. During migration times, larger birds such as storks and birds of prey can be seen almost anywhere flying overhead. For peace and quiet in Marrakech visit the Jardin Agdal, the Jardin Majorelle or the Jardins Mamounia. In Casablanca visit the Parc de la Ligue Arabe on avenue Hassan II and in Tanger visit the Jardin du Mendoubia.

The Middle Atlas

Driving south from Fès, travellers soon come to the mountain range of the Middle (Moyen) Atlas. The terrain and vegetation is far from uniform: high, stony plateaux, lakes and wonderful cedar forests all grace this area and are rich in wildlife. Ifrane, Azrou and Midelt make good bases from which to explore the area. In spring and early summer, the cedar woods – particularly good around Ifrane – have a lush understorey of colourful flowers including numerous orchids, cistuses, fritillaries and narcissi. Butterflies such as cleopatras, large tortoiseshells and fritillaries visit the flowers, and the woods are home to troops of Barbary apes. One of the special birds here is Moussier's redstart. These elegant little birds are resplendent in black, white and red plumage and are sometimes surprisingly tame. The stony plateaux are the domain of jackals as well as birds such as larks, pipits and wheatears. Long-legged buzzards and Egyptian vultures sometimes float overhead, and lizards and scorpions shelter under stones in the heat of the day. The lakes to the east of Ifrane provide a contrasting habitat, with many species of waterbird as well as frogs and terrapins. Ifrane lies 31 miles (50km) south of Fès on the P24; continue on this road to reach Azrou. The lakes or 'dayèts' can be reached along minor roads east from Ifrane – Dayèt Aaoua is at the junction of the P24 and the 4627. Also try the 3325, 4630 and 4632 to reach dayèts Hachlaf, Ifrah and Afourg.

The High Atlas

Snow-capped in winter, the High (Haut) Atlas mountains dominate central Morocco.

...a stork en route *to other climes*

Although largely inaccessible, the higher reaches of the Atlas National Park can be explored from the Tichka Pass between Marrakech and Ouarzazate and the ski resort of Oukaïmeden, while the southern foothills can be explored by following the valleys of the Dadès and Todra rivers.

To reach Oukaïmeden, drive south from Marrakech via Aït-Lekah; the ski resort lies on the 6040.

The gorges of the Dadès and Todra offer dramatic scenery, together with varied birdlife which changes with increasing altitude. At lower levels, white storks, great grey shrikes, common bulbuls and, during migration times, swallows, can be found around cultivated land. However, once the terrain becomes rocky, look for blue rock thrushes, Barbary partridges, Moussier's redstarts and rock buntings. Even if you

PEACE AND QUIET

do not see any of these, you will be unlucky indeed not to see the lizards that abound here. To reach the Dadès Gorge turn north on the S6901 at Boumalne-Dadès on the P32. The Gorges du Todra turning is at Tinerhir (Tineghir) on the P32; take the S6902.

Deserts

Although, to some people, deserts are barren and lifeless places, in reality they support a surprising range of creatures. Each is superbly adapted to life in this harsh, arid environment

Fint Oasis, near Ouarzazate

and the very fact that they can survive in such inhospitable conditions is a wonder in itself. For visitors captivated by the unique magic of the desert, both stony semi-deserts and the wind-blown sands on the fringes of the Sahara are waiting to be explored. One of the more accessible areas can be found to the south of the road (P32) between Tinejdad and Er-Rachidia and further south to Erfoud and Rissani. Exploration of the desert further afield should not be attempted without a four-wheel drive vehicle and the aid of a guide.

Desert mammals such as fennec fox, jackal and addax (a kind of antelope) are usually only seen by luck or chance. The birdlife includes an impressive array of larks and wheatears to test the birdwatcher's identification skills; stony desert habitat is more likely to yield results than bare sand.

The road from Er-Rachidia to Erfoud runs along the course of the Oued Ziz. The lush vegetation and palm groves here provide an interesting alternative to the desert. Ouarzazate is another good base from which to explore the desert. Of special interest is the El-Mansour-Eddahbi reservoir, which attracts wintering wildfowl and acts like a magnet to migrating waders and storks.

Merdja Zerga

The lake of Merdja Zerga in the Moulay-Bousselham Reserve lies on the Atlantic coast of Morocco, north of Rabat between Larache and Kénitra. Although interesting at any time of year, the area is probably of most interest to the birdwatcher in winter, when thousands of wildfowl and waders appear, and during migration times when almost anything could turn up. The appearance of a few slender-billed curlews in the winter months is a major attraction to dedicated birdwatchers from all over Europe. This is a threatened and endangered species and seldom seen anywhere else nowadays. It resembles a small curlew with a shorter bill, pale

Birds of Merdja Zerga	
In winter	
wigeon	black-tailed godwit
mallard	dunlin
shelduck	Kentish plover
spoonbill	redshank
flamingo	
At migration time:	
black-winged stilt	
avocet	
wood sandpiper	
Caspian tern	
whiskered tern	
white stork	
little egret	
cattle egret	

eye-stripe and neatly spotted underparts.

To reach Merdja Zerga, take the P2 to Souk el Arba du Rharb and then turn west on the S216A to Moulay-Bousselham. Tracks and roads lead around the lake.

Lac de Sidi Bourhaba

On the Atlantic coast north of Rabat and just inland from Mehdiya, Lac de Sidi Bourhaba is a delightful wetland reserve. Although the southern half of the lagoon has restricted access, most, if not all, of the interesting species that it harbours can be seen from the road around the northern section. In common with other undisturbed lakes and lagoons on the Moroccan coast, large numbers of wildfowl are attracted here during the winter months, and in migration periods waders, terns, egrets, flamingos and birds of prey pass through.

PEACE AND QUIET

This is also one of the few remaining sites left in Morocco for African marsh owls, putting it on the itinerary of most keen birdwatchers. To stand the best chance of seeing one you will have to stay until dusk, when they begin quartering the lake margins. With distant views and in poor light, beware of confusing them with marsh

A perching tawny eagle

harriers, which sometimes continue flying until late in the evening.

Among the other special birds that you might see here are marbled ducks. These are among Europe's most endangered species of duck; several hundred of them are likely to be here during the winter. As their name suggests these ducks have a boldly marked and mottled plumage, with large cream-coloured blobs against a chocolate background. The region is home not just to birds. Spur-thighed tortoises plod through the undergrowth in early spring and you may even spot a chameleon camouflaged among the vegetation.

To reach Lac de Sidi Bourhaba turn off the P29 approximately 18 miles (30km) north of Rabat on the S212 to Mehdiya. Just before the village, the road runs around the lake.

Sous Valley

Nestling between the mountain ranges of the High Atlas and the Anti-Atlas inland from Agadir, the Sous valley comprises rich agricultural land with olive groves, orchards and cultivated fields. However, some areas of natural habitat, particularly forest, still persist. Although these have been degraded by livestock – the goats are adept at tree-climbing – there are still some good areas, and in these can be found a wide range of unusual Moroccan birds. Stone curlews, although secretive and well camouflaged, can be found by persistent scanning through binoculars, but Moussier's redstarts, common bulbuls, rufous bushchats and black-headed bush shrikes should be easier to see. Keep an eye on the skies above for birds of prey such as short-toed eagles, tawny eagles and long-legged buzzards.

Black-shouldered kites, arguably the most elegant of Morocco's raptors, can also be found in the Sous valley. Since they habitually perch on bare branches, good views can often be obtained.

To reach the Sous valley, take

Drama in the High Atlas: sun setting the Dadès Gorge aflame

the P32 inland from Agadir, then minor roads to Aoulouz.

Agadir

Agadir makes an ideal base for birdwatching. Not only can good sea watching be had up and down the coast, but inland lies the Sous valley with its agricultural plains and forests. However, a major highlight is undoubtedly the area where the Sous wadi meets the sea just to the south of Agadir. The estuary and surrounding marsh and scrub are a superb area for birdwatchers, indeed for observing local wildlife in general.

On the mudflats and sandbanks of the Sous look for waders, including black-winged stilts during migration times (March and April and September and October). No one is ever likely to confuse these extraordinary birds with any other. Not only are they startlingly black and white in plumage, they also have dead-straight needle bills, and to cap it all impossibly long, thin legs – the longest, in comparison to their body size, of any bird.

Storks, spoonbills and egrets are also common and, in the winter months, there is even a chance of seeing a bald ibis. The latter species is one of the most threatened birds in the world, with Morocco harbouring all but one of its breeding colonies – there is still a small colony near Aoulouz.

Oued Massa

The point where the Oued Massa reaches the sea to the south of Agadir is one of the most outstanding coastal

PEACE AND QUIET

birdwatching sites in Morocco. Sandbars effectively turn the mouth of the river into a lagoon and a track on the northern shore allows excellent views across the whole area. Although there is something of interest throughout the year, birdwatching is best during the winter months and, more especially, during spring and autumn migration.

During the winter, Oued Massa is home to thousands of coots and ducks; gull and tern flocks are always worth close inspection for unusual species, and a highlight of this season is the presence of wintering flocks of cranes. As an added bonus, bald ibises feed at Oued Massa and a few individuals can usually be seen at any time of year.

Migration times see the arrival of huge numbers of birds on their journey north, many of which stay to feed and rest for a few days. Waders, egrets, herons, swallows and bee-eaters are among the highlights, and an impressive list of European breeding birds can be built up in a short while. In the surrounding scrub and arid land, look for black-bellied sandgrouse, which come to the water to drink each morning, stone curlews, cream-coloured coursers, crested larks and black-crowned bush shrikes. Chameleons can sometimes be found in the vegetation, and skinks, agama lizards and Barbary ground-squirrels scurry for cover.

To reach the mouth of Oued Massa, drive south from Agadir on the P30 and turn west towards Arhbalou and then northwest to Sidi-Rbat. Park and explore the area on foot.

Bird Migration

Morocco is on a major migration route for birds which winter in West Africa and breed in Western Europe. A major reason for its strategic importance is that most landbirds try to minimise the amount of open Mediterranean Sea they have to cover by using the narrow Straits of Gibraltar to cross between the two land masses. Although visible migration can be seen almost anywhere given the right time of year and the correct weather conditions, the Tanger peninsula is particularly favoured for witnessing mass migrations.

Sea bird migration can be seen almost anywhere along the Moroccan coast, although huge numbers of Cory's shearwaters, Manx shearwaters, gulls and terns are funnelled through the Straits. However, it is the large day-flying migrants, such as birds of prey and storks that are particularly noticeable. Species frequently seen include black kites, lesser kestrels, Montagu's harriers, sparrowhawks and hobbys as well as white storks. When winds are from the west, spring migration is most noticeable along the eastern side of the Tanger peninsula and when blowing from the east, migration is from the west. In the autumn, birds come in off the sea almost anywhere.

FOOD AND DRINK

Food

Freshness is the key to a delicious, little-known cuisine, whose repertoire is as varied in origin as the Moroccans themselves. Fish, meat and vegetables are rarely more than a day old, sometimes only a matter of hours. The food markets in the major cities are a canvas of vivid colour and plenty, accompanied by subtle aromatic smells.

Moroccan food, one of food writer and expert Robert Carrier's favourite topics, is based on sheep and vegetables, and flavoured both with the spices of the Orient and the subtleties of French cuisine. By the sea there are also mounds of fresh sardines, shrimps, prawns, mussels, squid and a host of larger fish, as well as oysters, particularly at Oualidia.

Pâtisseries abound and are very popular. Most Moroccan sweets include almonds or honey, the most famous being *cornes de gazelle*, 'gazelles' horns'. These are small, croissant-shaped pastries filled with almond paste. Cafés also serve croissants and *pains au chocolat* for breakfast. Lorries on the roads groan beneath the burden of a variety of seasonal fruits. From October there are dates in the south, and throughout the winter a range of oranges, clementines and satsumas.

Picnics

Bread, tomatoes, cucumber, olive oil, tuna fish, sardines,

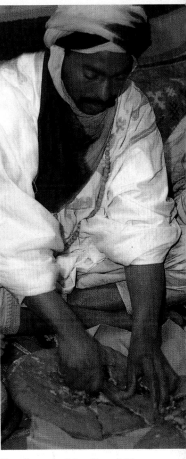

One slice or two? Local hospitality is as good as the food

oranges, dates and mineral water can all be bought at the large urban markets and carried away in a woven raffia basket. For wine, beer, cheese and salami, you will probably have to go to a local supermarket, though the major city markets also have delicatessen stalls which sell these.

Eating Out

There are three main categories of restaurant in Morocco. Cheapest are the street-hawkers and small **grill-cafés**, which serve brochettes, kebabs of either liver or meat in bread, hard-boiled eggs sprinkled with cumin, finely chopped, fiery salads, chicken and *harira*, a thick, nourishing soup. These vendors tend to cluster in the medina and round the bus and railway stations, and to operate at particular speed on market days, when clusters of low, earthenware pyramidal pots steam outside over charcoal braziers. These contain *tajines*, a stew which can be one of the most sublime taste experiences in Morocco. Usually composed of a little mutton and a mound of root vegetables, *tajines* are simmered slowly for hours in a little olive oil, their own juices and an infinitely varying combination of spices, and eaten with chunks of fresh bread.

Tajine also features in the country's greatest restaurants, exclusively in the cities, where prices may equal those of Europe. Here the *tajine* may be made with fish, spiced meat-balls, young lamb and prunes or chicken, deliciously infused with the flavours of lemon and olives. Other specialities of *haute cuisine* are often distinguished by a subtle juxtaposition of sweet and savoury tastes. *Bastilla*, for example, is a spiced pigeon pie encased in flaky pastry and sprinkled with sugar and cinnamon. The dish which Moroccans eat for celebrations at home is couscous, also available in the better restaurants. It is often bland outside the home however, and if anyone offers to cook you couscous at home take up the offer. At its best it is a fluffy pile of semolina-like pasta, heaped with spicy vegetables and meat, served with additional juices. At some restaurants you can order *mechoui* in advance, though it is mostly prepared at festivals and for larger, group meals. A whole lamb is slowly spit-roasted or prepared in an oven to melt in the mouth.

The third category of restaurant comes in between, is usually found in the French new towns, and often suffers from a schizophrenic dual personality. These restaurants are the descendants of colonial favourites, which continue to serve an essentially French menu, camouflaged by years of local interpretation and the addition of a number of watered-down local dishes. Only a few of them are worth visiting and they are recommended in the body of the guide. The same is unfortunately true of a lot of the hotel food, so eating out is well worth the effort.

Drinking

Alcohol is discouraged by Islam, and bars are few and far between outside the tourist hotels. Those that do exist are usually hidden down back streets and in the newer part of towns, and cater to an exclusively male clientele, not often a relaxing environment for Western women.

When choosing a restaurant, bear in mind that the cheaper grill-cafés and restaurants in the medina and restaurants in the countryside are unlikely to serve alcohol. When travelling in the south, it is advisable to buy your own supply if you like an evening drink, as it is not sold outside Agadir and Ouarzazate. Delicious bottled mineral water, *Sidi Harazem* or *Sidi Ali*, or the fizzy *Oulmès*, is available everywhere, and street-hawkers, cafés and restaurants also serve freshly squeezed orange juice. But the Moroccan staple drink is mint tea, normally served with a surfeit of sugar. Though excessively sweet to the European palate, it is excellent in hot weather to give an injection of energy.

Moroccan Wine and Beer

Vineyards established by the French continue to produce white, red and rosé wine. The reds are excellent but strong, suitable for drinking with a meal, the best labels being *Cabernet President* and *Amazir Beni M'Tir*. For a refreshing aperitif, try a chilled *Gris de Boulaouane* or *Oustalet* rosé, for Morocco's white wines are rather acidic. With seafood, try the white *Special Coquillage*, however. For those who prefer beer, the best of the local brands of lager is *Flag Special*.

SHOPPING

The souk, or market place, lies at the heart of each Moroccan community. In the big cities it is made up of a labyrinthine web of narrow streets, each specialising in a particular trade. In the countryside, a designated patch of land is transformed once a week into a tented city, selling everything from camels to marriage costumes to the surrounding villagers. Though there are no set hours, trading in the towns begins early, knocks off in the heat of the day and reaches a frenetic pitch in the early evening.

Buying and Bargaining

The guile of Moroccan tradesmen, and of the local guides who lead tourists into the market place in pursuit of a commission, knows few bounds. Morocco is full of appealing buys, but the objects first proffered to you will be of dubious quality and astronomic price. Early trips to a government-run Centre Artisanal and to a museum of local crafts to get an idea of prices and quality is good ammunition with which to enter the fray.

As for bargaining, which you will be expected to do, it was originally devised as a method of establishing a price with which both parties were happy, and it is up to you to bring this about. To be sure that it happens, first decide exactly what you want, how much or how many. Secondly, make up your mind what you are prepared to pay for it. Thirdly, stick to both of these resolutions, and do not be deflected by the inclusion of a free 'gift', by the kind offer of mint tea which you may certainly accept, or by any attempt to make you feel unreasonable. Few visitors have ever beaten the locals at their game, so be ruthless!

Crafts
Though rarely of premier quality, Moroccan craftwork is original and attractive.

Carpets
Tetouan, Fès, Meknès, Rabat and Marrakech all have acres of carpet bazaars, cascading with miles of knotted carpets, woven killims, prayer mats, cushions and killim bags. The carpet wares produced by the tribes of the Atlas mountains are of most interest, because of their authentic, traditional Berber designs.

Leatherwork
This is everywhere, in the form of wallets, pouffes (large cushions), bags, pointed slippers, belts, cigarette cases and desk sets. The best quality slippers are usually in suede or heavily embroidered, a fact that is reflected in the price.

Metalware
Every bazaar offers trays and table tops, lanterns and candelabra, pistols, daggers and teapots in brass or silver. Casablanca is one of the main centres for metalwork.

Pottery
Ubiquitous, also is a dazzling display of ceramics: bowls, ashtrays, *tajine* pots and

Everything for the slippery customer

candlesticks. At Safi the potters produce the most brilliant rich glazes, while Fès is long renowned for its blue and white designs.

Silver and Jewellery
These are best bought in the south, particularly at Tiznit, but unless you are an expert beware – the materials may not be what you think.

Woodwork
This, in the form of polished boxes, inlaid chess and backgammon sets and even table tops is traditionally the skill of the carpenters and woodcarvers of Essaouira on the Atlantic coast.

Fossils and Minerals
Fossilised fishes embedded in polished black stone, massive ammonites, slivers of brightly

coloured quartz, pieces of amethyst and lustrous, carved stone eggs are regularly touted on roadsides in the south. Avoid the bright red and green crystals, whose fake dye is detectable at first sight.

Local Specialities

The spice markets are heaped with many-coloured powders, like bowls of traditional paint pigments. Among the red chilli, golden turmeric and ochre cumin nestles green powdered henna, which gives a deep red sheen to hair and is also used to decorate the hands and feet of local women for important celebrations. Near by are native apothecaries, selling variously coloured kohls, twigs for tooth cleaning and remedies for all forms of impotence. Tubs of olives cured with lemon juice, peppers and garlic, and olive oil itself, are also difficult to resist.

ACCOMMODATION

Except for the very cheapest, all Morocco's hotels are star rated and carefully inspected by the government. Any Tourist Office, in the country or abroad, will give you a complete list covering all hotels from five-star Luxe to one-star B. It also lists campsites and includes information on hotel facilities such as swimming-pools, gardens, air conditioning and the number of rooms.
At the top end of the scale there are hotels like Winston Churchill's favourite, La Mamounia in Marrakech. Hidden behind the ochre city walls, it is an opulent palace with gardens, fountains and hot-and-cold-running staff. Most of the more expensive hotels recommended in the guide are in the four-star bracket, which guarantees supplies of water, efficient plumbing and hygiene for a reasonable price. The cheaper recommendations are normally clean, plain, often family run and friendly. An increasing number of self-catering apartments are being built in the seaside resorts, particularly in Agadir, and should be booked through a tour-operator. If you are looking for cheaper accommodation be aware that unclassified hotels can be both unsafe and unsanitary. Always check the room before booking into a hotel. (See **Tight Budget** for further information and for Youth Hostels.)

A wandering minstrel entertains the crowds in Marrakech

Due to the climate, water supply in the cheapest hotels outside the resorts is sporadic, affecting not only the state of the lavatories but also of general cleanliness. A lack of water provides a great excuse to go and try the local hammam or Turkish bath. Since few Moroccans have their own, these public baths are widely used, and for the traditional women they are a centre for social life and an exchange of local gossip. The hotel reception will be able to direct you.

ENTERTAINMENT AND NIGHTLIFE

At sunset, a magical cocktail of smells and music heralds the start of the evening's festivities. Particularly during Ramadan, when darkness signals the end of the fast, the streets and squares of cities and towns throng with snack-food stalls, musicians and story-tellers, and the souks reverberate to noisy commercial transactions.

No one should miss one of the world's great public spectacles on place Jemaa el Fna, Marrakech, the setting for a mushrooming city of hawkers, snake-charmers, quack doctors, fortune-tellers and tented kitchens, all illuminated by flickering gas lights.

In addition to the street life, Morocco offers a couple of unique evening entertainments. Restaurants established in old Moorish palaces serve traditional meals to the accompaniment of music, folk dancers, belly dancers, acrobats and fire-eaters. At evening 'fantasias', easily arranged from hotels in Agadir, Marrakech or Tanger, traditional food is served in open-sided tents, before a spectacle which climaxes with an explosive, musket-firing horse-back stampede.

Returning to any of the large hotels after your meal, the disco is in full swing, often hosting cabaret turns late into the night. If you want to go on the town, the larger cities also have independent nightclubs and a casino as well.

WEATHER AND WHEN TO GO

The ideal time for a general visit to Morocco is in the spring, when rain is unlikely and the heat not yet debilitating. Springtime wild flowers, ripening crops and migrating birds brighten hills and agricultural regions which are parched in the summer. At the same time both the Atlantic and Mediterranean are warm enough to swim in. Autumn (late September to early November) brings another mild period, particularly suitable for walking in the higher mountains.

Unless you intend to do very little but sunbathe, swim and siesta or go into the mountains, avoid the high summer – June, July and August.

Anywhere south of Agadir on the coast, and inland in the desert, the heat is blistering and the most active period of local life is between 04.00 and 07.00 hrs. This region is best explored in the winter, coinciding with the frantic activity of both the date and olive harvests, and when the mostly clear, sunny skies make a therapeutic change from the grey of northern Europe. Elsewhere in winter there is a danger of rain, and the Mediterranean resorts are almost deserted.

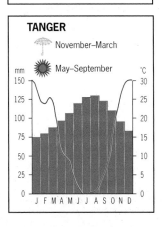

AGADIR

☂ November–February

☀ March–September

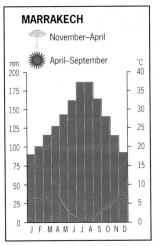

MARRAKECH

☂ November–April

☀ April–September

TANGER

☂ November–March

☀ May–September

Protection from the sun is a must...

What to Wear

Whenever you visit, take a sun hat and dark glasses. Temperatures drop markedly at night, particularly in the desert, and a thick jersey and socks are vital in winter. A light waterproof coat would also be useful. For the rest of the year a series of thin layers, which you can shed and re-apply, is a good idea. Take a light sweater too, for the chilling effect of too much sun or the occasional cool evening.

HOW TO BE A LOCAL

The differences between Moroccan and Western culture are more than skin deep, but for a start do not expose too much flesh. Moroccans are now used to bikinis and shorts on the beach, but in towns and near holy places it is extremely offensive to show much thigh, breast or upper arm. Men should wear cotton trousers and short-sleeved shirts, women flowing skirts and loose shirts. Forget the boob tubes and tight black numbers to show respect to your host country.

Covering the body is just one of many codes of conduct which come from Morocco's Islamic and Arab heritage. This heritage also teaches a tradition of hospitality which far exceeds our own. The Arabs respond to such hospitality with effusive thanks, at a level that is hard for Westerners to attain. Be as fruity as you want with your praise, and perhaps give a gift if you have something suitable.

Entering a Moroccan home, you should take your shoes off. If food is prepared for you but no implements are provided, use the bread as a tool and eat with your right hand – the left is traditionally used for ablutions after the lavatory. It is sad, but women of the house are unlikely to eat with you, even if your party includes Western women.

Another tradition of Islam concerns beggars, for the Koran enjoins Muslims to give 'what you can spare' to them. Collect change to distribute, and you will be following the Muslim religion closer than many of the locals seem to. Morocco is also a good place to come off alcohol for a while. The locals drink pints of refreshing mint tea and freshly squeezed orange juice.

CHILDREN

The family occupies an important position at the centre of Moroccan life, and as a result children are highly prized. Travelling with children here is a good way of making friends. However, children should never be let out of parents' sight.

The large resorts, and package holidays, are more likely to provide specific children's activities. Most of the large hotels offer baby-sitting services, and also have shallow pools for children. On a few beaches donkey or camel rides are available. In Agadir there is a miniature train to ferry you around the town, and in Marrakech there is a fleet of horse-drawn carriages. Even at Agadir with its calm sheltered bay, swimmers should always beware of the Atlantic waters, whose currents and undertow are powerful and dangerous. Of all the country's many sites, three may be of special interest to children:

Museum of Military Miniatures, Palais Mendoub, Tanger. An enormous and bizarre collection of toy soldiers, amassed by American publishing millionaire, Malcolm Forbes, in his palace overlooking the sea.
Open: daily 10.00–17.00 hrs.
Ouzoud Waterfall (Cascades d'Ouzoud), between Beni-Mellal and Demnate, northeast of Marrakech. Plummeting 300 feet (100m) among quasi-tropical vegetation and miraculous rock formations, water from the Ouzoud river

…here local style has a head start

forms a series of natural swimming-pools below. In summer they are the focus for a tourist encampment.
Témara Zoo, south of Rabat. This is not up to Western standards, so do not take sensitive children. Playground facilities are included.
Open: daily 10.00 hrs–dusk.

TIGHT BUDGET

Travel

A large percentage of Morocco's tourists visit the country precisely because it is cheap. In winter, if you dare, wait until the last minute to book your flight, when prices to Agadir fall to rock bottom. In summer, availability is less predictable, and a bus ticket from Eurolines (leaving from London or Paris) may prove

TIGHT BUDGET

*Budget competition for shanks'
pony*

cheaper. Flights from the US
and Canada are expensive.
Travellers from North America
can take APEX flights (advance
booking essential) for much
less than the standard fares.
Once in Morocco, you will find
that hitching is most successful
out in the country, where
sporadic bus services have
bred communal tendencies.
You will probably be asked to
pay, as all the passengers do,
but do so at the end of your
journey. Otherwise, bus travel
is the cheapest at little over
£1/$2 per 60 miles (100km). It is
also a good way of meeting
people.

Accommodation
A list of the country's campsites
is available from Tourist Offices,
and there are Youth Hostels at
Asni, Azrou, Ifrane, Rabat,
Casablanca, Fès, Marrakech
and Meknès. Hotels in the
medina areas tend to be the

cheapest, but women travelling
alone or in pairs are advised to
spend a little more, in a one-star
establishment.

Eating
Fresh ingredients at the market
are very cheap and a loaf of
bread costs only one dirham so
midday picnics are ideal.
Buying wine, usually stocked by
supermarkets, is no cheaper
than in Europe, and restaurants
with licences tend to serve
more expensive food. Eat off
street stalls and at local grill-
cafés instead. In out-of-the-way
places, Moroccans will offer a
bed for the night, and prepare
mounds of steaming couscous
in your honour, for which
nothing is expected but the
blessings of Allah. Give fulsome
thanks, however, and a small
present from home is always
welcome.

In Brief

- Travel out of season
- Use local buses
- Eat at street stalls of grill-cafés
- Accept local hospitality

SPECIAL EVENTS

As well as the national holidays listed in the **Directory** (page 119), Morocco hosts a plethora of colourful events associated with the celebration of harvests, local saints' days, called moussems, and larger thematic festivals. They are made up of 'fantasias' (see page 108), singing, dancing and commerce. For exact dates, many of which are fixed at a local level, ask at any Moroccan Tourist Office:

Late February Tafraout: Almond Blossom Festival.
May Immouzer-Ida-Outanan: Honey Festival.
May/June El-Kelaa-Mgouna: Rose Festival.
Early June Marrakech: National Folklore Festival.
June Sefrou: Cherry Festival.
June Goulimine: Asrir Moussem.
August Setti Fatma, Ourika: Moussem of Setti Fatma.
August Asilah: Intellectuals' Moussem and Horse Festival.
Late August Sidi Ahmed ou Moussa: Acrobats' Festival.
September Agadir: Festival of African Music.
September Meknès: Fantasia Festival.
September Imilchil: Marriage Festival of the Aït Hadiddou.
September Moulay-Idriss: Moussem of Moulay Idriss I.
October Erfoud: Date Festival.

SPORT

Morocco's climate has encouraged good outdoor sports facilities. **Football** comes near to being an obsession among young men, with club games kicking off around lunchtime on Sundays and endless games on beaches and in town squares. **Tennis** is also popular. Courts abound in the resorts, often floodlit for playing in the cool of the evening. Of the more unusual sports, Morocco offers:

Fishing

Both sea fishing and fresh fishing in lakes and streams is available. Permits are required for the latter, from the local branch of the Administration des Eaux et Forêts. Hotel receptionists will be able to steer you in the direction of expert local advice and tackle. Down at Ad-Dakhla on the southern Atlantic coast, 100lb (50kg) corbina (a local game fish) have been landed by unsuspecting tourists.

Golf

Golf courses have proliferated since the first one was built in Tanger in 1917. The best courses – with 18 holes – are the Royal Dar-Es-Salam, Rabat; the Royal Course, Mohammedia; the Royal at Marrakech; and the Royal Country Club at Tanger. There are also 9-hole courses at Casablanca, Cabo Negro, Meknès and also at Agadir, where 18-hole and 9-hole courses are now open.

Hunting

The hunting season, for anything from partridges to wild boar, is during the winter. For further information contact **Sochatour**, 72 boulevard Zerktouni, Casablanca (tel: (02) 277513), who can arrange everything including guides and permits.

Riding

Apart from on the beaches, riding opportunities are quite hard to track down. Agadir and Casablanca both have stables, and La Roseraie Hotel, Ourigane, organises treks of up to a week in the Toubkal National Park in the High Atlas mountains.

Skiing

Morocco's main ski resort is in the High Atlas, at Oukaïmeden, about one hour from Marrakech. It has some of the world's highest lifts, up to 13,000 feet (4,000m), ski-rental and other facilities. Less taxing skiing is to be had near Ifrane in the Middle Atlas. Unfortunately, snow is rarely dependable in these southern climes, but the skiing season is normally from December to April.

Watersports

Sailing, windsurfing and scuba diving are available at all the major coastal resorts. Around Agadir, the surfing is particularly good, and few flights out there are complete without an Australian or two heaving a surf-board. Always remember the dangerous currents and undertow when playing in the Atlantic.

Agadir beach is a magnet for all sorts of sports enthusiasts

DIRECTORY

Arriving
By Air
The national airline of Morocco is **Royal Air Maroc**, which has direct scheduled flights to Moroccan airports from London Heathrow, Paris and other cities in France (the French routes are shared with Air France). New York and Montreal also have direct flights to Morocco.

Royal Air Maroc Addresses:
London: 205 Regent Street, London W1R 7DE (tel: (0171) 439 4361).
US: 666 Fifth Avenue, 53rd Street, New York (tel: (212) 974 3850).
Canada: 1001 De Maisonneuve Ouest, Suite 430, Montreal (tel: (514) 285 1435).

There are international airports close to all the main resorts. They are much less garish, more utilitarian places than their European counterparts, but are equipped with a bank for changing money and a bar and souvenir shop in which to spend it. If you arrive on a package holiday, there will be a coach to meet you. Otherwise fleets of taxis and local buses wait at the entrance to all airports, or you can hire a car from one of the rental desks in the concourse.

By Sea
If you are driving or coming overland across Europe, the most frequent ferries to Morocco run between Algeciras in Spain and Tanger or Spanish Ceuta, on either side of the Straits of Gibraltar. Crossing the border from Ceuta into Morocco is often a lengthy process, so you should weigh up the marginally cheaper and quicker sailing against delays on land. Less frequent boats leave Spain from both Almeria and Malaga, docking in Spanish Melilla, a decaying hell-hole on the North African coast from which escape is also tediously bureaucratic.

Entry Formalities
Holders of valid Australian, British, Canadian, New Zealand

and United States passports are granted an automatic three-month visa at Moroccan borders. The same is true for all EU countries except Belgium and Holland, citizens of which should check with the Moroccan consulates in their countries before leaving. Temporary, visitors' passports are not accepted. Israeli and South African stamps no longer prohibit entry.

Only if you are arriving from an area of endemic yellow fever will you be asked to produce a certificate of inoculation. Driving your own vehicle, you must have the vehicle registration document, a valid EU, British or International driving licence and an international Green Card (insurance certificate), available from your insurers on request. At the border you will be able to buy third party insurance if your Green Card is not valid for Morocco.

Camping

Many of the inhabitants of Morocco live at least part of the year in tents themselves, and in summer entire families quit the cities for a month's camping by the sea, grandmother, babies and all. A network of campsites has developed, both on the coast and at the main holiday destinations inland, most of them equipped with electricity points for caravans. Some of the sites are idyllic, perched on cliffs above empty beaches, or shaded in palmery gardens, but in the larger cities you might consider a cheap hotel room preferable. All the campsites

are listed in the Moroccan Tourist Office's *Guide des Hôtels*.

If you are not camping in official sites, ask permission from the landowner, and do not be surprised if the police arrive asking you to fill in a permit.

Chemists
(see **Pharmacies**)

Crime

Unemployment and low wages mean that there is considerable poverty among Moroccans. They are certainly less affluent than visitors from the West. It is hardly surprising therefore to find tourists the object of pickpockets and hustlers. However, if you keep a close watch on your possessions in public, including on the beach, you should be safe. Crime rarely turns violent.

It is wise to note that almost all the worst holiday crime stories that come back from Morocco involve drugs.

Possession of the particularly strong marijuana, or kif, which is grown mainly in the Rif mountains in the north is illegal. The majority of its salesmen are not to be trusted and may well take advantage of your stoned state.

Customs Regulations

The usual allowances apply for spirits (1 litre) and tobacco (200 cigarettes), and you are officially allowed to take one camera, one video camera, one portable typewriter and one radio cassette player with you into the country. If you are

driving a car, you may import it free for six months, but if you sell it or keep it longer extortionate duty will be payable. Even if you write it off, you are still obliged to take it out of the country.

Disabled People
Facilities for disabled visitors are scarce, and few of the new package hotels even have lifts. **RADAR**, 12 City Forum, 250 City Road, London EC1U 8AF (tel: (0171) 250 3222) publish a booklet with suggestions for disabled people in Morocco, and **Creative Leisure** (tel: (0171)-235 2110) have experience of planning holidays there for wheelchair-users.

Car drivers should be careful of the rights of other road users

Driving
(see also **Arriving – Entry Formalities**)

Car Rental
Renting a car, from a Renault 4 (ideal for rough terrain) to a Mercedes, is easy but expensive. As well as the international agencies there are also cheaper local firms. Before accepting any car, check you have the vehicle registration certificate and insurance document, that the tyre tread is sufficient and that the spare is in good order.
Fuel prices are about the same

Light on the tiles in Casablanca

as in the UK (much higher than in the US), and though petrol stations are well distributed, in the south you should always fill up before leaving town. Road signs accord with international usage, and are modelled on the French.

Regulations and Suggestions
Once you are on the road keep to the right and remember that vehicles from the right have priority, so give way to those coming on to a roundabout. Try to avoid driving at dusk, when the light is difficult and everyone is on the move. Moroccan children have little traffic sense, and rush into the middle of the road unexpectedly, and both cyclists and horse carts can be unpredictable. Traffic and

narrow streets can make driving in cities a nightmare. Park your car and explore on foot. Flat tyres are the most common hazard, but can be repaired in most villages. If anything worse goes wrong, you are in good hands. Moroccan mechanics have been performing the impossible on their cars for years.

Electricity
Though there are still some areas of 110-volt electricity, most of the country is now served by 220 volts. Most plugs are round, two-pin, so an adaptor is advisable.

Embassies and Consulates
Australia: c/o Canada.
Canada: 13 Zankat Jaafar Es Sadik, Rabat (tel: (07) 771476).
New Zealand: c/o UK.
Republic of Ireland: c/o UK.
UK: 17 boulevard de la Tour Hassan, Rabat (tel: (07) 720905); consulate at rue Amérique de sud, Tanger (tel: (09) 935897); 60 boulevard D'Aula, Casablanca (tel: (02) 221653).
US: 2 avenue de Marrakech, Rabat (tel: (07) 762265); consulate at 8 boulevard Moulay Youssef, Casablanca (tel: (02) 224149).

Emergency Telephone Numbers
Police: 19
Ambulance: 15
Doctor: telephone hotel reception or local pharmacy.

Entertainment Information
To plan nightlife and day trips, consult your hotel reception or

visit the local Tourist Office, who will be able to inform you about any nearby festivals. Both regularly organise trips to fantasias and offer evening excursions to Moorish palace restaurants.

Health

(see **Arriving – Entry Formalities** for immunisation requirements.)
Though not essential, for peace of mind it is a good idea to be up to date on typhoid, cholera, tetanus and polio immunisation. The south of the country is allegedly home to malarial mosquitoes and bilharzia worms, and some visitors take malaria pills and avoid swimming in oasis pools or streams. Your doctor will be able to advise you on the current situation.
Though pharmacies are well-supplied, drugs are expensive and it is wise to bring a supply

Village women washing pots

of pain-killers, something to stem diarrhoea, and a remedy against sunburn.

Holidays (Public and Religious)

New Year's Day: 1 January
Feast of the Throne: 3 March
Labour Day: 1 May
Allegiance Day: 14 August
Day of Green March: 6 November
Independence Day: 18 November.
As well as this calendar of national holidays, Morocco observes the traditional feast days of the Muslim year as well, and the prescribed month of fasting, Ramadan. The most important feast days are Mouloud (the Prophet's birthday), Aid es Seghir, the 'small feast' (which ends Ramadan) and Aid el Kebir, the 'great feast'. The dates of these change each year as they follow the lunar calendar, occurring approximately eleven days earlier year by year.

DIRECTORY

Lost Property

Lost property offices do not exist in Morocco, but if you leave something behind in a hotel or a tourist restaurant, there is a good chance it will have been kept for you. If you wish to claim recompense for lost property on your travel insurance, go to the police to obtain a written report.

Media
Newspapers

English papers and the US's *International Herald Tribune* are available in all cities, with good selections in Tanger, Agadir and Marrakech New Town. French papers are even more widespread. Two of the Moroccan papers have a French edition, though both, *Le Matin du Sahara* and *L'Opinion*, toe the government line.

Radio

The BBC World Service broadcasts from 05.00 to 23.00 hrs on a bewildering variety of frequencies. The best are 12.095mhz (24.80m) in the early morning and during the evening, and 15.070mhz (19.91m) or 17.705mhz (16.94m) during the day.

Television

Local channels broadcast in Arabic, but there is a French news service.

Money Matters

The Moroccan dirham (DH) is divided into 100 centimes, and is issued in 200, 100, 50 and 10 dirham notes and coins of 5, 2 and 1 dirhams and 50, 20, 10 and 5 centimes.
Eurocheques are accepted in at least one bank in each major city, usually the SGMB, Société Générale Marocaine des Banques (see **Opening Times**), and both hotels and banks will change cash and travellers' cheques. Only the Banque Crédit du Maroc can make foreign exchange deals on Visa and Access cards, which are otherwise accepted in hotels, restaurants and shops.

The import and export of dirhams is illegal, since it is a 'soft' currency, the rate being set by the government independent of the world market. Budget carefully towards the end of your stay and keep your exchange slips as on departure you will only be allowed to reconvert half of what you can prove to have changed.

Opening Times
Banks

Normal banking hours are Monday to Friday 08.30–11.30 and 15.00–17.30 hrs. Banks are closed weekends and public holidays. During Ramadan, banks are open 08.30–14.00 hrs.

Post Offices

Post Offices (PTT) are open 08.30–12.00 and 14.30–18.30 hrs for postal services, while the attached international telephone offices stay open until 21.00 hrs.

The opening hours for **museums**, **sites** and **tourist offices** vary, but as a rough guide you should visit between 09.00–12.00 and 15.00–18.00 hrs. Many are closed on Friday mornings and all day Tuesday.

A bazaar display of metal work

Personal Safety

The most pervasive threat to visitors in Morocco comes from **the sun**, said to shine for 350 days a year, which burns easily, even in winter. Sun and after-sun creams are available.

The sun's natural partner, **the desert**, is also deceptively dangerous. If you are driving yourself in the south, always take a large jerry-can of water (enough for 8 pints (4.5 litres) per person per day), and never leave the designated roads. If you break down, or are halted by a sand storm, stay with your car as you are many times more likely to be found on the road than elsewhere on the unforgiving plateau. Never camp in a dry river bed, or wadi, as rain in the mountains miles away hurtles into the desert with unannounced ferocity, and has taken many a life. When the desert rivers are in spate, accept the offer of local help in crossing them. Western **women** are bound to come across Moroccan would-be Romeos, but it is rare for their attentive pestering to become physically threatening. You can help yourself by not walking alone at night or wearing provocatively scanty clothing. Hotel bedrooms in Morocco, even in some of the cheapest hotels, are usually safe places to leave your possessions.

Pharmacies

All towns have knowledgeable French-speaking, and sometimes English-speaking pharmacists. They sell bandages and antiseptics, and

DIRECTORY

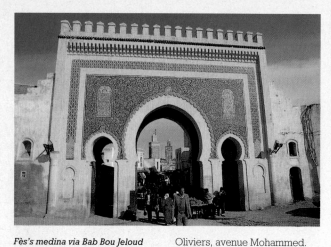

Fès's medina via Bab Bou Jeloud

drugs for common ailments such as diarrhoea, flu and sunburn, as well as contraceptives, but it is the general stores which sell tampons, soap and shampoo. If the pharmacist feels he cannot deal with your complaint, he will recommend a local doctor.

Places of Worship

There is just one working **Anglican** church, on rue d'Angleterre in Tanger. In Casablanca, there are **Catholic** services in English at the Church of Sainte Jeanne d'Arc, boulevard Moulay Youssef. French Catholic masses are held at:
Agadir: Eglise Sainte-Anne, rue de Marrakech.
Casablanca: Eglise Notre-Dame de Lourdes, place de l'Europe.
Fès: Eglise Saint-François, avenue Mohammed-es-Slaoui.
Marrakech: Eglise des Saintes-Martyres, rue El-Iman-Ali.
Meknès: Eglise Notre-Dame des Oliviers, avenue Mohammed.
Rabat: Cathédrale Saint-Pierre, place Al Katidraliya.
Tanger: Eglise Notre-Dame de l'Assomption, rue de Washington.
There is also a **synagogue** in Tanger, on boulevard Pasteur as well as several elsewhere in Morocco.

Police

Moroccan police come in two uniforms, the deep green of the Gendarmerie and the grey of the Sûreté. The **Gendarmerie** are quasi-military, largely concerned with national security on sensitive borders or in anarchic regions such as the cannabis-growing Rif mountains. The regular crime-busters and law enforcers, the **Sûreté**, are armed, but it is to them you should report crime.

Post Office

There are post offices, known by the French acronym PTT, in every Moroccan town (see also **Opening Times**). They sell stamps, send telegrams and receive Poste Restante mail should you have an address during your stay. They are also the cheapest and most efficient places from which to telephone abroad. Long queues for the phones betray the country's slow exchange, and you should slip the number you want on a piece of paper to the operator as soon as you arrive. Letter boxes throughout the country are yellow.

Public Transport
Air
Royal Air Maroc operates a full schedule of internal flights between the country's principal cities, particularly useful across the huge, dull distances in the Western Sahara, between Agadir, La'youne and Ad-Dakhla.

Buses
Several buses a day connect Morocco's main cities and towns, and are an invaluable place to meet genuine locals rather than just those who hang around tourist resorts. The national bus company, CTM, runs a fleet of smart, modern buses on a regular schedule, competing with a host of older (sometimes ancient) and cheaper privately owned buses. From each central bus station there is also a network of local departures covering almost all the nearby villages. ONCF, the rail company runs buses to connect with the rail service.

Trains
There are essentially two railway lines in Morocco, one from Tanger in the north to Marrakech in the south, the other between coastal Casablanca and Oujda on the Algerian border. In summer the air conditioning of first class is worth paying for, though generally second class, costing little more than a bus ticket, is comfortable enough.

Taxis
There are *grands-taxis* and *petits-taxis*, distinguished not only by size but also by destination. *Grands-taxis* operate like minibuses, touting for business in the taxi park and driving six passengers at high speed between principal towns. The price of a place in one of these is a little more than by bus. *Petits-taxis* are confined to towns and cities and to carrying three passengers. As the meters seldom work, agree a price with the driver before the journey begins.

Ferries
(see **Arriving**.)

Senior Citizens
The winter weather from Agadir south is invariably sunny, and attracts many retired people, who can live here warmly and more cheaply than they could at home. Many Continental Europeans spend the entire season in campervans on the sea-cliffs, though the beach-front hotels also offer good rates for long-stay guests. Anyone with mobility problems should check carefully on hotel facilities before booking, as most hotels do not even have

lifts or ramps for wheelchairs.

Student and Youth Travel

By and large, a student card is redundant plastic, having no effect on museum entrance prices and little on travel tickets. Royal Air Maroc do give a 25 per cent discount to those under 26 on their internal flights, but that is still a lot more expensive than bussing it. European InterRail passes, again for under 26s, extend to the Moroccan rail system.

Telephones

Morocco's telephones are nothing to call home about, and it is best to go to the nearest Post Office and ask the operator there to get you a line (it may take a long time). If you try on your own, dial 00 for an international line then 1 for Canada and the US, 44 for the UK, 61 for Australia, 64 for New Zealand and 353 for the Republic of Ireland, followed by the local code and number. When phoning Morocco from abroad, the country code is 212, preceded by the relevant international code (011 from the US and Canada, 010 (00 from 16 April '95) from the UK, 0011 from Australia, 00 from New Zealand and 16 from the Republic of Ireland).
Local calls are easily made from coin boxes, which accept 10, 20 and 50 centimes and 1 DH coins. Area codes are displayed in phone boxes or on a nearby wall. For information on telephone numbers, ring 186.

Emergency Numbers (see page 118).

Time

During the winter months, Morocco is on Greenwich Mean Time, but in summer the clocks are put forward an hour, at dates which do not coincide with the UK. In winter therefore, Morocco is five hours ahead of New York time, in summer, six.

Tipping

A service charge is usually added to restaurant bills but, like anywhere, a few extra dirhams will insure a good reception with the waiter next time. When parking in a town, there will always be someone to keep an eye on the car for 1-2DH. Otherwise museum and site guides, barmen, hairdressers, porters and petrol pump attendants will appreciate a tip, though taxi-drivers do not expect them.

Toilets

Morocco's smart hotels and restaurants are all equipped with flushing toilets, though the heat and sometimes a lack of water can spoil the hygienic effect. In local cafés and restaurants, toilets are the hole-in-the-ground variety, sometimes spotless with a cistern and foot pads, sometimes just a hole and a tap, for both washing and sluicing. Most Moroccans think toilet paper extremely unhygienic and always wash themselves using their left hand. You should therefore carry your own supply with you.

Tourist Offices

The Moroccan National Tourist Office (ONMT) have offices

throughout Europe and North America, where you can pick up leaflets and advice.
UK: 205 Regent Street, London W1 (tel: (0171) 437 0073).
Canada: 2001 Rue Université, Suite 1460, Montreal H3A 2A6 (tel: (514) 5562191).
US: 20 East 46th Street, Suite 1201, New York 10017 (tel: (212) 557 2520).
In Morocco itself, there are Tourist Offices in all main towns, and smaller Syndicats d'Initiative at lesser sites. Both are usually well-stocked with colourful local maps and brochures, and will advise you on local transport and the dates of the country's major festivals.
Agadir: place Prince Héritier Sidi Mohammed (tel: (08) 822894).
Casablanca: 55 rue Omar Slaoui (tel: (02) 271177), or 296 boulevard Mohammed V (tel: (02) 221524).
Essaouira: place Moulay El Hassan (tel: (04) 474172).
Fès: place de la Résistance (tel: (05) 623460), or place Mohammed V (tel: (05) 624769).
Marrakech: 170 avenue Mohammed V (tel: (04) 432097), or place Abdelmoumen ben Ali (tel: (04) 448906).
Meknès: place Administrative (tel: (05) 524426).
Ouarzazate: boulevard Mohammed V (tel: (04) 882485).
Rabat: rue Aguelmane Sidi Ali (tel: (07) 773644).
Tanger: 29 boulevard Pasteur (tel: (09) 938240), or 11 rue Khalid ibn el Oualid (tel: (09) 935486).

LANGUAGE

Common Moroccan Terms

agadir communal hilltop granary
ain spring or waterhole
akbar great
Alouite ruling dynasty
Andalous Mulslim Spain
bab gate
Berber indigenous people of Morocco
borj fort
caliph successor to Mohammed
dar house
jbel mountain
erg area of sand dunes
fantasia dramatic display of horsemanship
fondouk merchants' hotel and stables round court
hadith collected sayings of Mohammed
Haj title of pilgrim to Mecca
haik cloth covering women in public
hammam public steam baths
henna red/brown dye used on hair, hands and feet
imam leader of prayers
kasbah citadel/castle/fortress
killim woven carpet
Koran holy book of Islam
koubba domed saint's tomb
ksar/ksour fortified village
Maghreb the North African Arab nations
marabout holy man and tomb
medersa residential Muslim teaching college
medina old, walled city
mihrab niche in mosque denoting direction of Mecca
minaret tower of mosque
Mohammed the Prophet and founder of Islam
moussem pilgrimage/festival
muezzin caller to prayer

oued river
Ramadan month of fasting
ribat fortified monastery
sidi sir, title given to saint
souk market
sufi Muslim mystic
wadi/oued dry river bed
zaouia sanctuary/college at
tomb of marabout

The language of commerce

Arabic

Morocco's first language is
Arabic, though 40 per cent of
the population still speak
Berber as well. The Moroccans
are excellent linguists, and as a
legacy of the colonial period
most of them also speak French
and some a little English and
also Spanish. Unless you are
fluent, you should be sure to
pick up a French phrasebook
before you go. However,
learning to use a few Moroccan
Arabic phrases is not only
polite but gives great pleasure
and creates goodwill in all
situations. The accents in the
following list denote the
stressed syllables.

wahà/la yes/no
minfàdlik please
shòkran/barakalaùfik thank you
mizèyen good
meshèe mizèyen bad
labès/salamalaỳkoom hello
ooach khbàrek? how are you?
labès fine
sbah el khir good morning
msa el khir good afternoon
leèla saieèda good night
b'slèmah goodbye (in the
name of God)
kebìr big
seghìr small
bsh hal? how much?
ghaleè bzef too expensive
èmshee go away

Numbers

Arabic numbers, the origin of
our own system, are based on
the symbols for 1–9. Familiarity
with their appearance will be
helpful in shops and elsewhere.

1 ‏١‏
2 ‏٢‏
3 ‏٣‏
4 ‏٤‏
5 ‏٥‏
6 ‏٦‏
7 ‏٧‏
8 ‏٨‏
9 ‏٩‏
10 ‏١٠‏

wahèd/jooj/tlàta/àrba 1/2/3/4
khàmsa/sètta/sèba 5/6/7
tmènia/tseud/àshera 8/9/10
hadàch/etnàch/tlatàch
11/12/13
arbatàch/khamstàch 14/15
settàch/sebatàch 16/17
tmentàch/tsatàch 18/19
ashrìn/tlatìn/arbaìn 20/30/40
khamsìn/settìn/sebaìn
50/60/70
tmanìn/tsaìn/mia 80/90/100
mitìn/tlàta mia 200/300
alef 1,000

INDEX/ACKNOWLEDGEMENTS

The Automobile Association wishes to thank the following photographers and libraries for their assistance in the preparation of this book.

PAUL KENWARD took all the photographs in this book (© AA PHOTO LIBRARY) except:

P CORY 69 Souks Marrakech.

INTERNATIONAL PHOTOBANK Cover Water seller, 10 Mosaics Volubilis, 23 Tanger, 27 Country scene, 37 Performers, 45 Casablanca Cathedral, 49 Granary, 75 Essaouira Harbour, 84 Imouzzer market day, 94 Arabs with camels.

NATURE PHOTOGRAPHERS LTD 100 Tawny Eagle (P R Sterry).

ZEFA PICTURE LIBRARY (UK) LTD 87 Taroudannt city walls.

Copy editor for original edition: Audrey Horne.
For this revision: Copy editor Jenny Fry.
Thanks also to Barnaby Rogerson for his updating work on this revised edition.